IDENTIFY THEM. CONFRONT THEM. CRUSH THEM.

WALK IN FREEDOM.

CRUSHING THE GIANTS

VOLUME 4

KINGDOM STRATEGIES FOR LEADERS AND CREATIVES IN ARTS & ENTERTAINMENT

DR. RENETTA S. WATSON

CRUSHING THE GIANTS

KINGDOM STRATEGIES FOR LEADERS & CREATIVES
IN ARTS AND ENTERTAINMENT

VOLUME 4

Dr. Renetta S Watson

DrRenettaSWatson@yahoo.com
314-312-3448
DrRenettaSWatson.com
CrushingTheGiants.com

Published by ACT Publishing
An imprint of A Caring Touch Design & Publishing
ACaringTouchPublishing.com

TABLE OF CONTENTS

INTRODUCTION

If this is your first *Crushing the Giants* book, welcome. You have picked up more than a book. You have picked up a battle plan.

Whether you realize it or not, there is a war taking place. It is not merely a war between people, organizations, cultures, or circumstances. It is a spiritual war that manifests in every area of life. It affects our thoughts, emotions, relationships, purpose, finances, health, calling, creativity, and legacy. Many people spend their lives fighting the wrong enemy. They attack people when the real battle is spiritual. They become frustrated with circumstances when something much deeper is influencing those circumstances. They attempt to solve spiritual problems with natural solutions and then wonder why the cycle continues. The purpose of the *Crushing the Giants* series is to expose the giants behind the battles so they can be identified, confronted, and ultimately crushed.

Throughout Scripture, giants represented obstacles that appeared bigger than God's people. They stood between individuals and the promises of God. They produced fear, intimidation, delay, discouragement, compromise, and defeat. Although the names and circumstances have changed throughout history, the enemy's strategy has not. Giants still exist today. Some are obvious, while others remain hidden beneath years of pain, disappointment, rejection, trauma, fear, or false beliefs. Some operate loudly, while others quietly influence our thinking, our decisions, our relationships, and our future without ever being recognized. One of the primary purposes of this series is to help you recognize that not every battle is the same because not every giant is the same.

Throughout these books, we discuss four different types of giants. There are personal giants that attack our minds, emotions, habits, beliefs, and behaviors. There are relational giants that seek to destroy marriages, families, friendships, churches, and communities. There are territorial giants that influence cities, cultures, organizations, and entire regions. Then there are generational giants, destructive patterns that travel through family lines until someone decides the cycle ends with them. Each type of giant requires discernment because each one must be addressed differently. Some giants are displaced by replacing lies with truth and unhealthy patterns with Kingdom principles. Some are dismantled through repentance, healing, and obedience. Others require deliverance, while still others simply lose their power when we stop feeding them. Every giant has a strategy, and God has given us a strategy for every giant.

One of the foundational principles of this series is understanding the difference between defeating a giant and crushing a giant. David defeated Goliath when he struck him with the stone, but he crushed

Goliath when he removed his head. There is a difference. Many people experience temporary victories only to find themselves facing the same battles again because they defeated the symptom but never dealt with the source. A defeated giant can often return in another form, but a crushed giant loses its authority to continue ruling your life. God's desire is not simply that you survive your battles. His desire is that you experience lasting transformation and permanent freedom.

Another foundational truth we explore throughout this series is how giants are created. Giants rarely appear overnight. Most are formed through mixture. Throughout Scripture, mixture represents combining what God intended to remain pure with something He never intended to coexist with it. It is faith mixed with fear, truth mixed with deception, purpose mixed with insecurity, obedience mixed with compromise, worship mixed with idolatry, or identity mixed with performance.

Over time, mixture produces confusion. Confusion produces bondage, and bondage eventually produces giants. One of the greatest works of the Holy Spirit is separating what has become mixed so that purity, clarity, healing, and freedom can be restored.

This series also recognizes a truth that many people overlook. The greatest attacks often come against those carrying the greatest assignments. Throughout the Bible, the enemy consistently opposed those who were called to build, create, write, lead, govern, teach, influence, and establish God's purposes in the earth. The enemy has always targeted vision because vision changes generations. That is why creatives often experience unusual resistance. Writers battle self-doubt before finishing the manuscript. Entrepreneurs face fear before launching the business. Leaders encounter criticism before influencing others. Ministers experience discouragement before preaching breakthrough. Innovators often meet resistance before introducing something new. The enemy rarely wastes energy attacking someone who carries no purpose. He attacks potential because he fears what God intends to accomplish through your life.

Volume Four focuses on some of the most internal giants people face. These are often the giants others cannot see. Many people smile publicly while privately battling anxiety. They faithfully serve while carrying unresolved grief. They are surrounded by people while quietly wrestling with loneliness. They know what God has promised, yet struggle with unbelief. They love God but wrestle with subtle forms of rebellion. They continue moving forward while carrying offenses they have never truly released. These giants often work beneath the surface, shaping our thoughts, influencing our decisions, affecting our relationships, and limiting our ability to fully embrace God's purpose for our lives.

We begin this volume with grief because loss has a unique way of affecting every other giant. Unprocessed grief can give strength to anxiety. Disappointment can produce unbelief. Isolation often deepens loneliness. Wounds can harden into offense. Pain that is never healed can eventually become rebellion. When grief remains unresolved, it creates fertile ground for other giants to grow. Yet God never intended for grief to become our permanent dwelling place. He heals the brokenhearted, restores what has been lost, and brings beauty from ashes.

As you journey through these pages, I encourage you to read prayerfully and honestly. Invite the Holy Spirit to reveal not only the giants you already recognize but also those that may have quietly influenced your life for years. Do not become discouraged if you see yourself in these chapters. Recognition is not defeat; it is the beginning of freedom. Every giant exposed loses some of its power. Every lie replaced with God's truth weakens the enemy's influence. Every act of obedience advances God's Kingdom within your life.

The battle is real. The giants are real. But God's promises are greater than every giant you will ever face. No wound is beyond His healing. No cycle is beyond His power to break. No life is too damaged for His restoration. As you turn these pages, my prayer is that you will not simply learn about giants, but that you will identify them, confront them with God's truth, receive His healing, and crush every obstacle standing between you and the destiny He has prepared for you.

Welcome to *Crushing the Giants, Volume 4*. The battle continues, but so does the victory. Let's begin.

GRIEF

Introduction: Grief Is Bigger Than Death

When most people hear the word grief, they immediately think about death. They think about funerals, cemeteries, tears, and mourning the loss of a loved one. While grief certainly includes those experiences, grief is much bigger than death.

Grief happens anytime there is a loss.

You can grieve the death of a person, but you can also grieve the death of a dream. You can grieve the loss of a marriage, the loss of a job, the loss of a ministry position, the loss of health, the loss of mobility, the loss of innocence, the loss of financial stability, the loss of identity, or even the loss of a season of life.

Some people are grieving who they used to be before trauma touched them. Others are grieving the life they thought they would have. Some are grieving because cancer took a breast, diabetes took a limb, depression took years, betrayal took trust, or divorce took the family they prayed would stay together.

Others are grieving transitions. A mother may grieve when her children grow up and no longer need her in the same way. A pastor may grieve when a season of ministry comes to an end. A business owner may grieve when they must close something they spent years building. A person can even grieve after answered prayer because every new season requires the death of an old one.

Grief is the emotional response to loss. It is the heart's response to change, disappointment, separation, transition, and pain. Whenever something meaningful is removed, grief often follows.

The problem is not grief itself. The problem occurs when grief is not processed properly. Left unaddressed, grief can become a giant. It can drain your joy, steal your passion, make you emotionally numb, and convince you that life will never feel whole again.

But grief was never meant to imprison you.

God never intended for you to carry grief forever. The goal is not to pretend the loss did not happen. The goal is not to suppress your emotions. The goal is not to simply get over it.

The goal is healing.

The goal is learning how to mourn without losing yourself. The goal is learning how to feel pain without allowing pain to become your identity. The goal is learning how to move through loss without allowing loss to permanently define your future.

Ultimately, the goal is crushing the giant of grief before grief crushes you.

What Grief Does

Grief affects every part of a person: spiritually, emotionally, mentally, physically, and relationally. It rarely stays contained in one area of life. Instead, it has a way of touching everything.

Grief can make you tired even when you have slept. It can make you angry without explanation. It can make you withdraw from people, lose your appetite, overeat, or lose interest in things you once enjoyed. It can create anxiety, depression, brain fog, irritability, insomnia, hopelessness, and emotional exhaustion.

Sometimes grief shows up as tears. Sometimes it shows up as silence. Sometimes it appears as frustration, impatience, or emotional numbness. Other times it disguises itself as busyness, overworking, perfectionism, or isolation.

Many people think they are crazy when they are actually grieving.

They wonder why they cannot focus. They wonder why they are so emotional. They wonder why they are angry all the time. They wonder why they feel disconnected from everyone around them.

What they often fail to realize is that grief affects the entire person.

Grief can also distort perception. It can make you question God, question yourself, and question your future. It can make you replay conversations, revisit painful memories, and struggle with decisions you have already made.

Unresolved grief has a way of leaking into every area of life. Unhealed grief can turn into bitterness, fear, emotional isolation, distrust, and anger toward people who did not cause the original pain. It can create walls where God intended healing. It can produce distance where God intended connection.

A person grieving the loss of a loved one may suddenly struggle with trust in other relationships. Someone grieving a divorce may become fearful of intimacy. Someone grieving the loss of a job may begin questioning their value and identity. Someone grieving the loss of health may begin struggling with confidence and self-worth. When grief remains unaddressed, it often multiplies into additional emotional battles.

This is why grief must be addressed both clinically and spiritually.

Clinically, we understand that grief affects the brain, emotions, and behavior. Spiritually, we understand that grief affects the soul. God created us as whole beings, which means healing must take place holistically. We cannot ignore the emotional while focusing only on the spiritual, nor can we ignore the spiritual while focusing only on the emotional.

True healing happens when both are addressed.

The reality is that grief is not a sign of weakness. It is evidence that something mattered. It is evidence that something valuable was lost. It is evidence that love, hope, trust, investment, or expectation existed.

The problem is not that grief exists. The problem is when grief becomes permanent residence.

God never intended grief to become your identity. He never intended pain to become your address. He never intended sorrow to become your future.

Grief is a season. A painful season. A necessary season. A human season. But it is still a season and seasons are meant to change.

The giant of grief wants to convince you that the pain will never end, that joy will never return, and that healing is impossible. But the truth is that grief can be processed, wounds can heal, and life can exist beyond loss.

You may never be the same person you were before the loss, but that does not mean your life is over. It simply means God must now heal, strengthen, and rebuild the parts of you that were impacted by what happened.

The goal is not to pretend the loss never occurred. The goal is not to erase the memory. The goal is not to deny the pain.

The goal is to learn how to carry the memory without carrying the weight. The goal is to remember without remaining trapped. The goal is to mourn without losing yourself. The goal is to heal. Healing is how we begin crushing the giant of grief.

Signs You Are Grieving

One of the most dangerous things about grief is that many people do not realize they are grieving. This is because grief does not always look like tears. In fact, some of the people carrying the deepest grief rarely cry in front of others. Grief is often misunderstood because people expect it to look a certain way. They expect sadness. They expect mourning. They expect visible pain. However, grief has many faces, and it often disguises itself as something else.

Sometimes grief looks like anger. Sometimes it looks like exhaustion. Sometimes it looks like silence. Sometimes it looks like emotional numbness. Other times it shows up as irritability, isolation, overworking, perfectionism, people pleasing, or completely shutting down emotionally.

Many people think they have an attitude problem when what they are actually carrying is unprocessed grief. Others believe they are simply stressed, frustrated, burned out, or emotionally detached when underneath all of it is loss that was never fully acknowledged.

Grief often wears disguises. It hides behind behaviors, reactions, and emotional patterns that seem unrelated to loss. Because of this, many people spend years trying to fix symptoms while never addressing the real issue. If you do not recognize grief, you cannot heal it. You cannot confront what you refuse to identify.

One of the clearest signs of grief is a change in your emotional responses. Things that normally would not bother you suddenly irritate you. Situations that once seemed manageable now feel overwhelming. You become more impatient, more emotional, more sensitive, and more reactive. Small frustrations trigger larger reactions because your emotional reserves have already been depleted.

Sometimes the opposite happens. Instead of feeling too much, you stop feeling altogether. You become emotionally numb, detached, and disconnected. You stop reacting because you have become emotionally exhausted. Some people cry over everything, while others cannot cry at all. Both can be signs of grief. Some become highly emotional, while others become emotionally unavailable. Both responses can be the result of loss.

Scripture tells us that "Hope deferred makes the heart sick" (Proverbs 13:12). Loss affects the heart, and when the heart is wounded, emotions often become unstable. What you are experiencing may not be weakness. It may not be a lack of faith. It may not be emotional immaturity. It may simply be grief.

Another sign of grief is anger. Many grieving people do not initially appear sad. They appear angry. This is because anger is often easier to express than pain. Pain feels vulnerable, but anger feels powerful. Pain makes us feel exposed. Anger makes us feel protected. As a result, many people hide behind anger because it feels safer than admitting they are hurt.

Instead of saying, "I'm hurt," "I'm disappointed," "I feel abandoned," or "I'm broken," people lash out. They become defensive, harsh, critical, impatient, and sometimes explosive.

They find themselves reacting strongly to situations that previously would not have affected them.

Sometimes the anger is directed at other people. Sometimes it is directed at God. Sometimes it is directed inward toward themselves. There are people who are not mean; they are grieving. There are people who are not difficult; they are carrying unresolved pain. There are people whose frustration is actually sorrow that has never been processed.

When grief is ignored long enough, it often hardens into bitterness. Ephesians 4:31 tells us, "Let all bitterness and wrath and anger and clamor and evil speaking be put away from you." Bitterness is often grief that stayed too long. It is pain that was never properly processed. It is hurt that was never healed.

Grief also changes behavior. People who once enjoyed being around others suddenly isolate themselves. They stop answering calls. They avoid social gatherings. They withdraw from relationships. Sometimes they do not have the energy to engage. Other times they simply do not want to explain what they are feeling.

People who were once disciplined may lose motivation. People who were once joyful may become cynical. Some people overeat while others stop eating altogether. Some oversleep while others cannot sleep at all. Some throw themselves into work because staying busy helps them avoid feeling. Others lose all productivity because the emotional weight becomes overwhelming.

Some people become emotionally clingy because grief creates a fear of additional loss. Others push everyone away because they are afraid of being hurt again. Grief affects people differently, but it almost always affects behavior.

Grief can also manifest physically. Fatigue, body aches, headaches, brain fog, forgetfulness, anxiety, panic attacks, and difficulty concentrating are all common responses to loss. Many people are surprised to learn that grief affects the body as much as it affects the emotions. The body often carries what the heart has not processed. Emotional pain frequently becomes physical discomfort.

Another significant sign of grief is mental replaying. You replay conversations, failures, moments, and regrets. You revisit events repeatedly in your mind, wondering if something could have been done differently. Thoughts such as "What if?" "If only..." and "I should have..." become common companions.

Your mind keeps revisiting the loss in an attempt to regain control over something that cannot be changed. This is especially common after divorce, death, job loss, trauma, failed relationships, ministry transitions, financial setbacks, health diagnoses, and major life changes. Unresolved grief often traps people in the past mentally and emotionally.

Many grieving individuals also struggle to move forward. Not because they do not want healing, but because part of them fears that moving forward means letting go. Some people unconsciously stay connected to pain because the pain feels connected to what they lost. They fear that healing means forgetting. They fear that joy means dishonoring what was lost. They fear that happiness somehow minimizes the significance of the person, relationship, season, or dream they are grieving.

But healing does not dishonor what was lost. Healing honors the fact that life still has purpose. Healing honors the fact that God is not finished with your story. Healing honors the truth that while loss may have happened to you, loss does not have to define you.

Recognizing grief is often the first step toward healing. Before you can crush the giant of grief, you must first identify it. You must recognize its voice, its symptoms, and its influence in your life. Only then can you begin the process of confronting it, processing it, surrendering it to God, and ultimately overcoming it.

Grief may be present, but it does not have to remain. What is recognized can be addressed. What is addressed can be healed. And what is healed no longer has the power to control your future.

The Five Stages of Grief

From a clinical perspective, psychiatrist Elisabeth Kübler-Ross identified five common stages of grief: denial, anger, bargaining, depression, and acceptance. These stages have helped countless people understand the emotional journey that often follows significant loss.

It is important to understand that grief does not always move in a straight line. People do not necessarily experience these stages in order, nor do they experience them only once. Someone may move from anger to acceptance and then back to anger again. Another person may experience several stages at the same time. Grief is personal, and every person's journey looks different.

These stages are not rules. They are road signs. They help us recognize where we are emotionally and understand that what we are feeling is often a normal response to loss.

Understanding these stages helps us identify the giant we are facing and equips us to move toward healing rather than becoming trapped in pain.

Denial: "This Cannot Be Happening"

Denial is often the first response to loss. It is the mind's attempt to protect itself from overwhelming emotional pain. When reality feels too painful to process all at once, denial acts like a temporary shield.

This is the stage where people struggle to accept what has happened. They may avoid conversations about the loss. They may avoid emotions. They may avoid facts that force them to confront reality.

Sometimes denial sounds spiritual.

"I'm fine." "It doesn't bother me." "I've moved on.""God's got it."

While faith is important, denial can sometimes hide behind spiritual language. There is a difference between trusting God and pretending you are not hurting.

The danger of denial is that buried pain does not disappear. It waits. Pain that is not processed does not leave. It simply goes underground until it resurfaces in another form. What is denied emotionally often appears later as anxiety, anger, bitterness, depression, physical symptoms, or unhealthy coping mechanisms.

Psalm 107:6 says, "Then they cried to the Lord in their trouble, and He delivered them from their distress."

Notice that deliverance came after acknowledgment. Healing begins when we stop pretending and start telling the truth. To crush the stage of denial, you must become honest about your loss. Give yourself permission to admit that something hurts. Stop minimizing what happened. Stop comparing your pain to someone else's pain. Loss is loss.

Speak honestly with God. Journal your thoughts and emotions. Talk with trusted people who create safe places for healing. Most importantly, allow yourself to feel what you feel without judgment.

You cannot heal what you refuse to acknowledge.

Anger: "Why Did This Happen?"

After denial begins to fade, anger often emerges.

Anger is one of the most misunderstood stages of grief because many people do not realize that anger is often a secondary emotion. Underneath anger is usually hurt, disappointment, fear, confusion, or sadness.

People may become angry with God. Angry with themselves. Angry with doctors. Angry with family members. Angry with church leaders. Angry with former spouses. Angry with employers. Angry with circumstances.

Sometimes they are angry because life feels unfair. They prayed and still experienced loss. They believed and still suffered disappointment. They trusted and still got hurt.

Anger is especially common after divorce, betrayal, abandonment, trauma, job loss, financial collapse, or unexpected tragedy.

Ephesians 4:26 says, "Be angry, and do not sin."

Notice that Scripture does not condemn the emotion of anger. God understands human emotion. The issue is not whether anger exists. The issue is what we do with it.

Anger can either become a bridge to healing or a prison of bitterness.

To crush this stage, do not weaponize your pain. Avoid taking your hurt out on people who did not cause it. Learn healthy ways to process emotion. Pray honestly. Seek counseling if necessary. Exercise and release physical tension. Give yourself permission to grieve without allowing grief to become aggression.

Forgiveness also becomes important during this stage. Forgiveness does not excuse what happened. It simply prevents what happened from continuing to control you.

Unprocessed anger eventually becomes poison.

Bargaining: "If Only..."

Bargaining is the stage where the mind begins replaying the past.

People revisit conversations, decisions, opportunities, and moments, searching for ways things could have been different.

"If only I had stayed." "If only I had called." "If only I had worked harder." "If only I had seen the signs." "If only I had gone to the doctor sooner." "If only I had prayed more."

Bargaining is the mind's attempt to regain control over something that can no longer be changed.

Unfortunately, guilt cannot rewrite history.

Many people remain stuck in this stage because they assume responsibility for things that were never fully within their control. They carry guilt for outcomes they could not prevent. They blame themselves for circumstances that involved many factors beyond their influence.

Philippians 3:13 reminds us, "Forgetting those things which are behind and reaching forward to those things which are ahead."

Paul is not suggesting that we erase the past. He is teaching us not to become trapped by it.

To crush the bargaining stage, you must release false responsibility. Accept that not everything was in your control. Stop trying to rewrite history. Give yourself grace. Trust God with unanswered questions. Some questions may never be answered on this side of eternity.

Healing begins when we stop living in "what if" and start living in "what now."

Depression: "I Don't Know How to Move Forward"

Depression is often the deepest and heaviest stage of grief.

This is where the reality of the loss settles in. The shock has faded. The anger has weakened. The bargaining has exhausted itself. The weight of what happened becomes undeniable. People lose motivation. They lose energy. They lose interest in things they once enjoyed. Simple tasks begin to feel overwhelming. Many describe feeling stuck, numb, hopeless, or emotionally exhausted.

This stage is especially dangerous because it is where the giant of grief often tries to establish permanent residence. People begin believing the pain will never end. They begin believing joy will never return. They begin believing their future has been permanently damaged.

Psalm 34:18 says, "The Lord is near to the brokenhearted and saves the crushed in spirit."

Notice that God does not distance Himself from brokenness. He moves closer to it.

To crush this stage, refuse isolation. Stay connected to healthy people. Seek professional support if needed. Maintain routines even when you do not feel like it. Take care of your physical body. Continue praying. Continue worshiping. Continue feeding your spirit.

Do not wait until you feel strong to do healthy things. Sometimes healthy actions help create healthy emotions. Depression whispers that nothing will ever change. But feelings are not always facts.

Acceptance: "This Happened, But It Will Not Destroy Me"

Acceptance is often misunderstood. Acceptance does not mean you are happy about the loss. It does not mean the loss no longer hurts. It does not mean you have forgotten.

Acceptance simply means you have stopped fighting reality. It means you have acknowledged what happened and chosen to move forward.

You may still cry. You may still miss what was lost. You may still have difficult days. But the loss no longer controls your identity. You are no longer trapped inside the trauma.

Isaiah 61:3 speaks of God's promise to give beauty for ashes, the oil of joy for mourning, and the garment of praise for the spirit of heaviness.

Acceptance is where healing begins to replace survival.

To crush this stage, embrace healing. Allow yourself to hope again. Build new routines. Reengage with purpose. Reconnect with healthy relationships. Begin dreaming again. Help others who are walking through similar pain.

One of the greatest signs of healing is when your pain stops being only about you and begins becoming a source of encouragement for someone else.

Healing does not mean forgetting. Healing means the wound no longer rules you. Acceptance is not the absence of grief. It is evidence that grief no longer has the final word.

The Spiritual Perspective of Grief

While clinical psychology helps us understand the emotional and mental aspects of grief, Scripture provides another perspective. Clinical tools help explain what we are experiencing, but God's Word helps us understand what Heaven has provided for our healing. The world often teaches people how to survive grief, while God teaches us how to surrender it. The world tells us to manage grief, but God tells us He will carry it. The world focuses on coping mechanisms, but God offers transformation.

This does not mean clinical tools are unnecessary. God often uses counselors, therapists, doctors, support systems, and healthy relationships as part of the healing process. However, grief is not only emotional; it is spiritual. There are wounds that counseling can help identify, but there are burdens that only Christ can carry.

One of the most powerful Scriptures concerning grief is found in Isaiah 53:4: "Surely He has borne our griefs and carried our sorrows." Most people read this verse quickly and miss the significance of the language. Yet every word in this passage paints a picture of what Jesus came to do on our behalf.

Notice the first phrase: "He has borne our griefs." The word *borne* means to carry something heavy. It gives the image of a burden being placed upon someone's back. Imagine carrying a heavy backpack filled with rocks. Every step becomes more difficult because of the weight you are carrying. Now imagine that backpack filled with grief. Inside that backpack are painful memories, disappointments, betrayals, regrets, unanswered questions, broken dreams, shattered expectations, and every loss you have experienced. Perhaps it contains the grief of losing a loved one. Perhaps it contains the grief of divorce. Perhaps it contains the grief of losing a ministry, a business, a friendship, a job, your health, or a season of your life. Every painful memory becomes another weight. Every disappointment becomes another stone. Every heartbreak becomes another burden. Over time the backpack becomes heavier and heavier until the weight begins affecting every area of your life.

You become tired emotionally, exhausted mentally, overwhelmed spiritually, discouraged relationally, and weary physically. Yet Isaiah says Jesus bore our griefs. He took the backpack. He carried what was crushing us. He carried the weight we were never designed to carry alone. This does not mean the loss did not happen. It means the burden of carrying the loss was never meant to rest entirely on your shoulders.

Then Isaiah says He carried our sorrows. The imagery shifts. The first picture is a burden carried on the back. The second picture is something carried in the hands. Psalm 56:8 provides a beautiful companion to this truth: "You number my wanderings; put my tears into Your bottle; are they not in Your book?" Think about that for a moment. God does not ignore your tears. He does not dismiss your pain. He does not overlook your heartbreak. Every tear matters to Him.

Every sleepless night, every silent cry, every private moment of sorrow, every painful memory, and every broken piece of your heart matters to God. The image is that of a loving Father collecting every tear and holding it carefully in His hands. He is not irritated by your grief. He is not impatient with your healing process. He is not frustrated by your pain. He carries it.

This means grief is not something you were designed to carry forever. The problem is that many people continue taking back what God already offered to carry. They pray about it and then pick it back up. They surrender it during worship and then pick it back up. They cry before God and then pick it back up. They place it at the altar and then carry it home again. Many believers spend years asking God to heal pain they refuse to release. Healing requires surrender. Healing requires trust. Healing requires exchange.

One of the reasons grief becomes such a giant is because people become attached to their pain. Sometimes pain becomes familiar. Sometimes grief becomes part of a person's identity. They no longer know who they are without the hurt. They become the widow, the abandoned spouse, the grieving parent, the betrayed friend, the unemployed worker, the wounded leader, or the person who suffered loss. The danger is that grief can move from something you experience to something you become.

Yet God never intended grief to become your identity. You are not your loss. You are not your heartbreak. You are not your disappointment. You are not your tragedy. You are not your pain. You may have experienced those things, but those things are not who you are. Grief may describe what happened to you, but it does not define who you are.

This is why healing requires more than surviving. Healing requires exchanging. Isaiah 61:3 gives one of the most powerful pictures of healing found anywhere in Scripture. God promises to give beauty for ashes, the oil of joy for mourning, and the garment of praise for the spirit of heaviness. Notice that everything in the passage involves exchange. Beauty for ashes. Joy for mourning. Praise for heaviness. God is offering something in place of what grief has stolen.

But an exchange only works when you release what you are holding. You cannot receive peace while gripping bitterness. You cannot receive healing while clinging to pain. You cannot receive joy while worshiping your wounds. You cannot receive restoration while refusing to release what was lost.

Many people wear grief like a garment. It becomes their identity, their personality, and eventually their entire outlook on life. But God says to take off the spirit of heaviness and put on a garment of praise. Take off despair and put on worship. Take off hopelessness and put on expectation. Take off bitterness and put on forgiveness. Take off fear and put on faith.

Praise does not deny pain. Praise simply declares that pain does not have the final word. Praise acknowledges that loss happened, but God is still faithful. Praise acknowledges that tears are real, but healing is available. Praise acknowledges that grief exists, but grief is not Lord. Jesus is.

The spiritual battle of grief is ultimately a battle of surrender. Will you continue carrying what Christ already carried? Will you continue holding what God is asking you to release? Will you continue identifying with your pain, or will you identify with His promises?

The cross did not remove every painful experience from life, but it did provide a place to bring every painful experience. The same Savior who carried the cross also carries grief. The same Savior who bore wounds also heals wounds. The same Savior who conquered death also has the power to help us overcome the losses we experience throughout life.

Grief may visit you, but it does not have permission to own you. The giant of grief may wound you, but it does not have the authority to define your future. Because what Jesus carries, He can also heal. And what you place in His hands, He has the power to carry away.

Signs You Are Grieving

One of the most dangerous things about grief is that many people do not realize they are grieving. This is because grief does not always look like tears. In fact, some of the people carrying the deepest grief rarely cry in front of others. Grief is often misunderstood because people expect it to look a certain way. They expect sadness. They expect mourning. They expect visible pain. However, grief has many faces, and it often disguises itself as something else.

Sometimes grief looks like anger. Sometimes it looks like exhaustion. Sometimes it looks like silence. Sometimes it looks like emotional numbness. Other times it shows up as irritability, isolation, overworking, perfectionism, people-pleasing, or completely shutting down emotionally. Many people think they have an attitude problem when what they are actually carrying is unprocessed grief. Others believe they are simply stressed, frustrated, burned out, or emotionally detached when underneath all of it is loss that was never fully acknowledged.

Grief often wears disguises. It hides behind behaviors, reactions, and emotional patterns that seem unrelated to loss. Because of this, many people spend years trying to fix symptoms while never addressing the real issue. If you do not recognize grief, you cannot heal it. You cannot confront what you refuse to identify.

One of the clearest signs of grief is a change in your emotional responses.

Things that normally would not bother you suddenly irritate you. Situations that once seemed manageable now feel overwhelming. You become more impatient, more emotional, more sensitive, and more reactive. Small frustrations trigger larger reactions because your emotional reserves have already been depleted.

Sometimes the opposite happens. Instead of feeling too much, you stop feeling altogether. You become emotionally numb, detached, and disconnected. You stop reacting because you have become emotionally exhausted. Some people cry over everything, while others cannot cry at all. Both can be signs of grief. Some become highly emotional, while others become emotionally unavailable. Both responses can be the result of loss.

Scripture tells us that "Hope deferred makes the heart sick" (Proverbs 13:12). Loss affects the heart, and when the heart is wounded, emotions often become unstable. What you are experiencing may not be weakness. It may not be a lack of faith. It may not be emotional immaturity. It may simply be grief.

Another sign of grief is anger. Many grieving people do not initially appear sad. They appear angry. This is because anger is often easier to express than pain. Pain feels vulnerable, but anger feels powerful. Pain makes us feel exposed. Anger makes us feel protected. As a result, many people hide behind anger because it feels safer than admitting they are hurt.

Instead of saying, "I'm hurt," "I'm disappointed," "I feel abandoned," or "I'm broken," people lash out. They become defensive, harsh, critical, impatient, and sometimes explosive. They find themselves reacting strongly to situations that previously would not have affected them.

Sometimes the anger is directed at other people. Sometimes it is directed at God. Sometimes it is directed inward toward themselves. There are people who are not mean; they are grieving. There are people who are not difficult; they are carrying unresolved pain. There are people whose frustration is actually sorrow that has never been processed.

When grief is ignored long enough, it often hardens into bitterness. Ephesians 4:31 tells us, "Let all bitterness and wrath and anger and clamor and evil speaking be put away from you." Bitterness is often grief that stayed too long. It is pain that was never properly processed. It is hurt that was never healed.

Grief also changes behavior. People who once enjoyed being around others suddenly isolate themselves. They stop answering calls. They avoid social gatherings. They withdraw from relationships. Sometimes they do not have the energy to engage. Other times they simply do not want to explain what they are feeling.

People who were once disciplined may lose motivation. People who were once joyful may become cynical. Some people overeat while others stop eating altogether. Some oversleep while others cannot sleep at all. Some throw themselves into work because staying busy helps them avoid feeling. Others lose all productivity because the emotional weight becomes overwhelming.

Some people become emotionally clingy because grief creates a fear of additional loss. Others push everyone away because they are afraid of being hurt again. Grief affects people differently, but it almost always affects behavior.

Grief can also manifest physically. Fatigue, body aches, headaches, brain fog, forgetfulness, anxiety, panic attacks, and difficulty concentrating are all common responses to loss. Many people are surprised to learn that grief affects the body as much as it affects the emotions. The body often carries what the heart has not processed.

Emotional pain frequently becomes physical discomfort.

Another significant sign of grief is mental replaying. You replay conversations, failures, moments, and regrets. You revisit events repeatedly in your mind, wondering if something could have been done differently. Thoughts such as “What if?” “If only...” and “I should have...” become common companions.

Your mind keeps revisiting the loss in an attempt to regain control over something that cannot be changed. This is especially common after divorce, death, job loss, trauma, failed relationships, ministry transitions, financial setbacks, health diagnoses, and major life changes. Unresolved grief often traps people in the past mentally and emotionally.

Many grieving individuals also struggle to move forward. Not because they do not want healing, but because part of them fears that moving forward means letting go. Some people unconsciously stay connected to pain because the pain feels connected to what they lost. They fear that healing means forgetting. They fear that joy means dishonoring what was lost. They fear that happiness somehow minimizes the significance of the person, relationship, season, or dream they are grieving.

Healing does not dishonor what was lost. Healing honors the fact that life still has purpose. Healing honors the fact that God is not finished with your story. Healing honors the truth that while loss may have happened to you, loss does not have to define you.

Recognizing grief is often the first step toward healing. Before you can crush the giant of grief, you must first identify it. You must recognize its voice, its symptoms, and its influence in your life. Only then can you begin the process of confronting it, processing it, surrendering it to God, and ultimately overcoming it.

Grief may be present, but it does not have to remain. What is recognized can be addressed. What is addressed can be healed. And what is healed no longer has the power to control your future.

The Great Exchange

One of the most powerful pictures of healing in all of Scripture is found in Isaiah 61:3. In this passage, God promises to give beauty for ashes, the oil of joy for mourning, and the garment of praise for the spirit of heaviness. While many people quote this verse, few fully understand what it means.

The entire passage is built around one word: exchange.

An exchange means that something is given up in order to receive something else. You cannot exchange something while continuing to hold onto it. You must release one thing before you can receive another.

This is where many people struggle in their healing journey. They want God's peace while holding onto bitterness. They want joy while clinging to sorrow. They want healing while refusing to release the pain. They want restoration while remaining emotionally attached to what was lost. Yet God's promise is built upon exchange.

He offers beauty for ashes. Ashes in Scripture often represent loss, devastation, disappointment, and mourning. Ashes are what remain after something has been burned. They represent what is left after dreams have died, relationships have ended, seasons have closed, and loss has occurred.

Many grieving people spend years sitting in the ashes of what used to be. The ashes of a marriage. The ashes of a ministry. The ashes of a friendship. The ashes of a career. The ashes of a dream. The ashes of a loved one. The ashes of who they used to be before trauma entered their lives.

God does not deny that the ashes exist. He simply offers something greater. He offers beauty in place of devastation. He offers restoration in place of ruin. He offers purpose in place of pain.

The exchange continues with the oil of joy for mourning. Mourning is a natural and necessary part of grief. God never condemns mourning. Jesus Himself mourned. The issue is not mourning. The issue is remaining permanently trapped in mourning.

There comes a point where God begins inviting us into healing.

The oil of joy does not erase the memory of what was lost. It simply means that grief no longer has complete control over your emotional life. It means you can smile again. Dream again. Hope again. Live again.

Finally, God offers a garment of praise for the spirit of heaviness.

Notice the imagery. A garment is something you put on intentionally. Praise is not always automatic.

Sometimes praise is a choice.
Sometimes praise is warfare.

When grief is heavy, praise becomes an act of resistance. When pain is overwhelming, praise becomes an act of faith. When tears are flowing, praise becomes a declaration that grief does not have the final word. Praise does not deny pain. Praise simply reminds pain that it is not in charge.

The Great Exchange is not a one-time event. It is often a daily decision. Every day we choose whether we will carry the ashes or receive God's beauty. Every day we choose whether we will live in heaviness or put on praise. Every day we choose whether grief will be our identity or whether healing will become our testimony.

The giant of grief grows stronger when we cling to what God is asking us to release. But every time we make the exchange, we weaken the giant's hold on our lives.

Grieving the Loss of a Season

One of the most overlooked forms of grief is the grief that accompanies the end of a season.

Most people associate grief with death. Yet many of life's greatest losses involve transitions rather than funerals.

Ecclesiastes 3:1 declares, "To everything there is a season, and a time for every purpose under heaven."

Life is filled with seasons. Some seasons arrive with excitement. Others end with sadness. Some transitions are welcomed. Others are painful.

A mother may grieve when her children grow up and no longer need her in the same way. A pastor may grieve when a ministry season closes. A business owner may grieve after selling a company they spent years building. A retiree may grieve the end of a career. A student may grieve the end of a chapter of life. A leader may grieve the loss of influence.

A person may grieve after moving away from a place that felt like home. Even positive transitions can create grief. This is why some people feel confused during seasons of promotion or answered prayer. They believe they should only feel excitement, yet they find themselves grieving.

The reason is simple: every new season requires letting go of an old one. There is often grief attached to what was familiar. You can celebrate the future while mourning the past. You can be excited about where God is taking you while grieving what you are leaving behind.

Both can exist at the same time.

Many people become emotionally stuck because they are trying to hold onto a season God has already closed. They continue living emotionally in a chapter that has already ended. They replay old memories. They compare every new experience to the old one. They romanticize what used to be. They resist what God is doing now because they are still attached to what He did before.

Yet every new level requires letting go of something old. Abraham had to leave. Moses had to leave. Israel had to leave Egypt. The disciples had to leave their nets.

Growth often requires departure. Part of crushing the giant of grief is accepting that not every season is meant to last forever.

Some seasons prepare you. Some seasons grow you. Some seasons teach you. Some seasons heal you. Some seasons launch you. Every season has an assignment, and every season eventually ends.

Healing begins when we stop trying to resurrect seasons God has completed and begin embracing the season He has placed before us.

The end of a season does not mean the end of your purpose. It simply means God is turning the page.

Grief and Physical Loss

One of the most personal and often overlooked forms of grief is the grief associated with physical loss.

When people think about grief, they rarely think about grieving the loss of a body part, physical ability, health condition, appearance, or level of independence. Yet for many individuals, these losses create profound emotional pain.

A woman may grieve after a mastectomy. A man may grieve after losing mobility. Someone may grieve after an amputation. Another may grieve infertility. Others may grieve chronic illness, disability, physical limitations, memory loss, or changes caused by aging.

These losses are unique because they often affect identity. People are not only grieving what was removed. They are grieving how life has changed because of what was removed. They grieve independence. They grieve confidence. They grieve normal routines. They grieve the future they expected. They grieve the version of themselves they once knew.

Physical loss often creates emotional questions. Will I ever feel normal again? Will people see me differently? Will I ever regain what was lost? Why did this happen to me? These questions are real, and they deserve honest acknowledgment.

Far too often people experiencing physical loss are encouraged to focus only on physical recovery while their emotional recovery is ignored.

Yet healing is not only physical. Healing is emotional. Healing is spiritual. Healing is psychological. Healing is relational. A person can recover physically while remaining emotionally wounded. This is why grief must be addressed.

The loss may have changed your body, but it did not change your value. Your worth was never based on what you could do. Your worth was never based on what you looked like. Your worth was never based on your physical abilities. Your worth was established by God. You are still fearfully and wonderfully made.

You are still created in the image of God. You are still valuable. You are still loved. You are still needed. You are still called. You are still worthy of dignity and honor.

The giant of grief wants people experiencing physical loss to believe they are less than they once were.

God says otherwise. The loss may have changed some things, but it did not change His purpose for your life. It did not change His love for you. And it did not change your value in His eyes.

Healing may look different than you expected, but healing is still possible. Hope is still possible. Joy is still possible. Purpose is still possible. Your story is not over.

Crushing the Giant of Grief

Understanding grief is important, but understanding alone does not produce healing. You can identify grief, recognize its symptoms, understand its stages, and even acknowledge its presence in your life while still remaining trapped by it. Information creates awareness, but intentional action creates freedom.

The giant of grief is not crushed simply because time passes. One of the greatest myths surrounding grief is the belief that time heals all wounds. Time alone does not heal wounds. Time only reveals what has and has not been healed. Some people have been grieving for six months. Others have been grieving for six years. Still others have been grieving for decades. The issue is not how much time has passed. The issue is whether healing has taken place.

Grief becomes dangerous when it stops being something you are processing and starts becoming something you are living in. God never intended grief to become your permanent residence. He never intended pain to become your identity. He never intended loss to become the lens through which you see your future.

To crush the giant of grief, you must first acknowledge the loss honestly. You cannot heal what you refuse to confront. Many people stay wounded because they spend years minimizing their pain. They say things like, "It wasn't that bad," "I should be over this by now," "Other people have it worse," or "I'm just being emotional." Yet every time they minimize their pain, they delay their healing.

Jesus asked blind Bartimaeus, "What do you want Me to do for you?" Not because Jesus lacked information, but because acknowledgment is often the first step toward healing. Healing begins when you tell the truth. You were hurt. You were disappointed. You were abandoned. You were betrayed. You suffered loss. Something valuable was taken, changed, broken, or ended. Until you acknowledge the wound, you cannot begin the healing process.

Part of crushing grief requires giving yourself permission to grieve. Many people feel guilty for grieving. They think grief is weakness. They think tears indicate a lack of faith. They think strong people should simply move on. Yet Scripture tells us that Jesus wept. If the Son of God could weep, then grieving is not weakness. Grieving is human.

Allow yourself to feel what you feel. Cry if you need to cry. Talk if you need to talk. Sit with the reality of the loss. Stop judging your emotions. Stop apologizing for your healing process. Grief is not evidence that something is wrong with you. Grief is evidence that something mattered.

Crushing the giant of grief also requires you to stop suppressing your emotions. Suppressed grief does not disappear. It stores itself. Eventually it leaks out through anger, depression, anxiety, addictions, control issues, perfectionism, emotional detachment, and bitterness. What you bury emotionally will eventually surface somewhere else.

Many people have become experts at hiding pain. They smile while hurting. They serve while hurting. They preach while hurting. They lead while hurting. They perform while hurting. But hidden pain is still pain. Strength is not emotional suppression. Strength is emotional honesty.

Ask yourself difficult questions. Am I angry, or am I hurt? Am I frustrated, or am I grieving? Am I exhausted, or am I carrying emotional weight that I have never released? Honest answers create pathways for healing.

Another critical step in crushing grief is separating your identity from your loss. One of grief's greatest dangers is identity attachment. People begin defining themselves by what happened to them. They become the divorced woman, the widow, the abandoned spouse, the grieving parent, the unemployed worker, the wounded leader, the cancer patient, or the betrayed friend.

Your experience is not your identity. You experienced loss, but you are not loss. You experienced pain, but you are not pain. You experienced disappointment, but you are not disappointment.

Jeremiah 29:11 reminds us that God still has thoughts of peace toward us and plans to give us a future and a hope. Grief may describe a season, but it does not define your destiny.

To crush the giant of grief, you must also release what you cannot control. A significant portion of grief comes from powerlessness. People replay conversations, revisit decisions, and imagine alternate outcomes because they desperately want control over something that cannot be changed.

Some questions will never be answered. Some situations cannot be reversed. Some people are not coming back. Some seasons are over. Acceptance is not weakness. Acceptance is wisdom.

Scripture instructs us to cast all our cares upon Him because He cares for us. Casting means throwing something off of yourself and onto someone else. Yet many people pray about their grief and then continue carrying it. They place it on the altar and then pick it back up on the way home.

Healing requires surrender. Not once. Daily. Sometimes hourly.

There are losses you will have to release repeatedly until your heart fully accepts what your mind already knows.

You must also embrace the Great Exchange. Isaiah 61:3 declares that God gives beauty for ashes, the oil of joy for mourning, and the garment of praise for the spirit of heaviness. Notice that every promise in the passage involves an exchange.

God offers beauty, but you must release ashes. God offers joy, but you must release mourning. God offers praise, but you must release heaviness.

Many people want God's healing without surrendering their hurt. They want restoration while continuing to cling to the pain. They want freedom while maintaining emotional attachment to what was lost.

But exchange only works when you release what you are holding. You cannot receive peace while gripping bitterness. You cannot receive healing while clinging to pain as identity. You cannot receive joy while worshiping your wounds.

Every day you must consciously choose the exchange. Take off despair and put on hope. Take off bitterness and put on forgiveness. Take off fear and put on faith. Take off heaviness and put on praise.

Praise does not deny pain. Praise simply reminds pain that it does not sit on the throne.

Another important part of crushing grief is rebuilding your life intentionally. Many people stop living after loss. They survive instead of live. They exist instead of engage. They function instead of flourish.

Healing requires rebuilding. You may need to rebuild confidence. You may need to rebuild trust. You may need to rebuild identity. You may need to rebuild routines. You may need to rebuild dreams. You may need to rebuild faith. Rebuilding is not weakness. Rebuilding is warfare.

Every healthy decision is an act of resistance against the giant of grief. Every step forward is a declaration that grief will not have the final word. Every prayer is resistance. Every counseling session is resistance. Every worship service is resistance. Every moment of choosing hope over despair is resistance. Every act of obedience is resistance. Every day you get back up is resistance.

Finally, allow God into the pain instead of only asking Him to remove it. Many people want God to instantly take grief away. Yet often God heals through process rather than immediate removal.

David said, “Yea, though I walk through the valley of the shadow of death.”

Notice he walked through it. Not around it. Not over it. Through it.

Some healing only happens while walking. Some healing only happens while trusting. Some healing only happens while surrendering.

God does not waste pain. He can bring wisdom from it, compassion from it, strength from it, ministry from it, and purpose from it.

Second Corinthians 1 teaches that God comforts us in our tribulation so that we may comfort others. Sometimes your healing becomes someone else's survival guide. Sometimes your testimony becomes someone else's roadmap out of darkness.

The giant of grief wants you emotionally paralyzed. It wants you trapped in yesterday. It wants you carrying burdens Christ already carried. It wants you convinced that healing is impossible.

Grief is not your destiny. Loss is not your identity. Pain is not your future. You can grieve and still heal. You can mourn and still move forward. You can cry and still have faith. You can experience loss and still experience joy.

Because the same God who bore your griefs and carried your sorrows is still carrying what you were never meant to carry alone. And what you place in His hands, He has the power to heal, restore, redeem, and carry away.

Prayers, Declarations, and Scriptures for Crushing the Giant of Grief

After grief has been identified, understood, acknowledged, and confronted, there comes a point where healing must be activated. Knowledge alone does not produce freedom. Information creates awareness, but prayer invites God into the healing process.

Throughout Scripture, people brought their pain, sorrow, disappointment, heartbreak, and loss before God. They cried. They lamented. They questioned. They worshiped. They prayed.

God never asked people to pretend they were not hurting.

He invited them to bring their hurt to Him.

These prayers and declarations are designed to help you release grief, receive healing, and partner with God in crushing the giant of grief.

Prayer for the Loss of a Loved One

Heavenly Father,

I come before You carrying the pain of loss. My heart hurts because someone I love is no longer here. There are memories, conversations, moments, and experiences that I wish I could relive. There are days when the pain feels overwhelming and nights when the silence feels heavy.

Lord, Your Word says that You are near to the brokenhearted and that You save those who are crushed in spirit. Draw near to me now.

Comfort me where I hurt.
Strengthen me where I am weak.
Heal the places in my heart that feel broken.

Help me grieve in a healthy way.
Help me to remember without

becoming trapped in sorrow. Help me to honor their memory without allowing grief to consume my future.

I surrender my tears to You. I surrender my questions to You. I surrender my pain to You.

Thank You for carrying what I cannot carry.

In Jesus' name,

Amen.

Scriptures for the Loss of a Loved One

Psalm 34:18, Matthew 5:4, Psalm 147:3, John 14:27, Revelation 21:4

Declarations

- I declare that God is near to me in my grief.
- I declare that I am not alone.
- I declare that healing is taking place in my heart.
- I declare that grief will not become my identity.

- I declare that God is carrying my sorrow and restoring my strength.

Prayer for the Loss of a Relationship or Divorce

Father,

I bring before You the pain of a relationship that has ended. You understand the disappointment, rejection, heartbreak, betrayal, and confusion that often accompany relational loss.

Lord, heal every wound left by broken expectations. Heal every place where trust was damaged. Heal every place where my confidence was shaken. Remove bitterness, resentment, unforgiveness, and anger.

Help me release what cannot be changed. Help me stop replaying the past. Help me stop carrying responsibility for things that were never mine to carry.

Teach me how to forgive. Teach me how to trust again. Teach me how to hope again.

I refuse to allow this loss to define my future. I place this relationship into Your hands. I release it. I surrender it. I trust You to redeem what I cannot repair. In Jesus' name,

Amen.

Scriptures for Relationship Loss

Psalm 147:3, Isaiah 43:18–19, Romans 8:28, Philippians 3:13–14, Jeremiah 29:11

Declaration

- I declare that my future is not determined by my past.
- I declare that rejection will not define me.
- I declare that God is healing my heart.
- I declare that bitterness has no place in my life.
- I declare that God has good plans for my future.

Prayer for the Loss of a Job or Financial Stability

Father,

You are my source. Jobs are resources, but You are my source. Businesses are resources, but You are my source. People are resources, but You are my source.

Lord, I confess that this loss has created fear, uncertainty, disappointment, and grief. But I choose to trust You.

Your Word declares that You shall supply all my need according to Your riches in glory by Christ Jesus.

I ask You to provide wisdom, opportunities, favor, open doors, and provision. Help me not to allow financial loss to become emotional defeat. Remind me that my value is not determined by my income. Remind me that my identity is not determined by my occupation. Remind me that You remain faithful.

I surrender financial anxiety. I surrender financial fear. I surrender financial grief. I receive Your peace.

In Jesus' name,

Amen.

Scriptures for Financial Loss

Philippians 4:19, Matthew 6:25–34, Psalm 37:25, Proverbs 3:5–6, Deuteronomy 8:18

Declarations

- I declare that God is my source.
- I declare that lack is temporary.
- I declare that God is opening doors.
- I declare that provision is coming.
- I declare that my future remains secure in God.

Prayer for the Loss of Health or Physical Ability

Father,

I bring before You the grief associated with physical loss, illness, disability, limitation, and change.

You understand the pain of losing abilities, independence, strength, mobility, health, or physical confidence.

Lord, heal my heart where loss has created sorrow. Help me not to measure my worth by what has changed physically.

Remind me that I am still valuable.
Remind me that I am still loved.
Remind me that I am still called.
Remind me that I still have purpose.

I reject the lie that my life is over because something has changed. I reject the lie that I am less valuable because of what was lost.

Help me discover joy again. Help me discover purpose again. Help me discover hope again. Thank You that my value comes from You.

In Jesus' name, Amen.

Scriptures for Physical Loss

Psalm 139:14, Isaiah 41:10, 2 Corinthians 12:9, Romans 8:28 Isaiah 40:31

Declaration

- I declare that my value comes from God.
- I declare that my purpose remains intact.
- I declare that God is strengthening me.
- I declare that hope is alive.
- I declare that my story is not over.

Prayer for the Loss of a Season

Father,

I bring before You the grief that comes with transition. I confess that part of me misses what was. I miss the people. I miss the familiarity. I miss the comfort. I miss the routines. I miss the season that has ended. But I trust that if You closed the door, You have a purpose for what comes next.

Help me release what You have completed. Help me stop living emotionally in yesterday. Help me embrace the new thing You are doing.

Give me courage to move forward. Give me faith for the next chapter. Give me peace in transition. I thank You that every season has purpose.

And I thank You that the end of a season is not the end of my story.

In Jesus' name,

Amen.

Scriptures for Transition

Ecclesiastes 3:1, Isaiah 43:19, Joshua 1:9, Proverbs 3:5–6, Jeremiah 29:11

Declaration

- I declare that God is leading me into a new season.
- I declare that I release what has ended.
- I declare that I embrace what God is doing now.
- I declare that my future is filled with purpose.
- I declare that God is turning the page and writing a new chapter.

Final Declaration Against the Giant of Grief

- Today I declare that grief will not control my life.
- I declare that grief is a season, not a destination.
- I declare that I will heal.
- I declare that I will hope again.
- I declare that I will dream again.
- I declare that I will trust again.
- I declare that I will live again.
- I declare that God has borne my griefs and carried my sorrows.

- I declare that I exchange beauty for ashes.
- I exchange joy for mourning.
- I exchange praise for heaviness.
- I declare that grief will not define me.
- Pain will not own me.
- Loss will not destroy me.
- The giant of grief is falling.
- The giant of grief is being crushed. And the God who carried my sorrow is leading me into healing, restoration, freedom, and joy.

In Jesus' name,

Amen.

UNBELIEF

Meaning

Doubt • Distrust • Misplaced Confidence • Negative Expectation • Agreement with Circumstances Over God's Word

Key Scriptures

Mark 9:23-24 - "Jesus said unto him, If thou canst believe, all things are possible to him that believeth. And straightway the father of the child cried out, and said with tears, Lord, I believe; help thou mine unbelief.

Hebrews 11:6 - But without faith it is impossible to please him: for he that cometh to God must believe that he is, and that he is a rewarder of them that diligently seek him."

Romans 10:17 - "So then faith cometh by hearing, and hearing by the word of God."

James 1:6-8 - "But let him ask in faith, nothing wavering..."

Ephesians 3:20 - "Now unto him that is able to do exceeding abundantly above all that we ask or think, according to the power that worketh in us."

Meet the Giant

Of all the giants we face, unbelief may be one of the most dangerous because it often hides in plain sight.

Unlike fear, anger, rejection, pride, or anxiety, unbelief rarely announces itself. It often disguises itself as wisdom, realism, caution, experience, or even maturity. Yet underneath these disguises is a silent agreement with something other than what God has said.

Within the Crushing the Giants framework, unbelief is often the hidden giant behind many other giants. Rejection survives because of unbelief. Fear survives because of unbelief. Anxiety survives because of unbelief. Poverty thinking survives because of unbelief. Stagnation survives because of unbelief. Even some forms of religion survive because of unbelief.

Unbelief causes people to agree with circumstances more than they agree with God. It causes people to trust their history more than His promises. It causes people to place greater confidence in what they have seen than in what God has spoken.

Many believers do not struggle because they lack information. They struggle because they have not fully believed the information they possess. The enemy understands something powerful: if he cannot stop God's promise, he will attempt to stop your belief in the promise. If he cannot change what God said, he will attempt to change what you expect.

This is why unbelief is so destructive. It affects every area of life. It affects how we pray, how we worship, how we lead, how we give, how we receive, how we dream, and how we respond to opportunities.

Many people have faith for salvation but unbelief for provision. Faith for heaven but unbelief for healing. Faith for eternity but unbelief for today. Faith that God can save their soul but uncertainty that He can restore their marriage, heal their body, bless their business, open a door, provide resources, or fulfill a promise.

The giant of unbelief attempts to shrink God until He fits within the limits of human experience. But throughout Scripture, God continually challenged people to see Him differently. He revealed Himself as Jehovah Jireh, the Lord our Provider; Jehovah Rapha, the Lord our Healer; El Shaddai, the All-Sufficient One; the God who parts seas, feeds multitudes, raises the dead, and calls things that are not as though they were.

The battle against unbelief is ultimately a battle over our picture of God. Because your expectation will never consistently rise above your revelation. If you see God as limited, your faith will be limited. If you see God as distant, your expectation will be distant. But when your revelation of God increases, your expectation increases, your faith increases, and your willingness to obey increases.

To crush unbelief, we must confront every thought, experience, disappointment, and belief system that exalts itself against the knowledge of God. We must learn to trust God's Word above our circumstances, God's character above our emotions, and God's promises above our past experiences.

A giant is not a sign to run. It is an announcement that you are standing in the vicinity of promise. And often, before we can conquer the giant in front of us, we must first crush the unbelief within us.

What Is Unbelief?

Unbelief is the refusal, inability, or struggle to fully trust what God has said, regardless of what circumstances appear to be saying.

Unbelief is not always atheism. Many believers love God and still battle unbelief. They believe God exists. They believe God can. They are simply not convinced that God will.

This is why unbelief is so dangerous. It often hides behind religious language while secretly expecting disappointment. It causes people to pray while expecting nothing. It causes people to worship while preparing for failure. It causes people to quote promises they do not actually expect to manifest.

Unbelief causes people to agree with circumstances more than they agree with God. It causes people to trust what they see over what God has spoken. The giant of unbelief attempts to make God's promises appear less real than your circumstances.

The Root of Unbelief

Unbelief often develops from disappointment. A prayer was not answered the way we expected. A relationship failed. A ministry opportunity closed. A loved one died. A business failed. A promise took longer than expected.

Over time people begin creating protective beliefs. They tell themselves, "If I don't expect much, I won't be disappointed."

Unfortunately, that mindset does not protect faith. It destroys it.

Many people are not struggling with God's ability. They are struggling with their expectations. They secretly expect disappointment because disappointment has become familiar.

What begins as disappointment can eventually become a belief system. A person may continue attending church, reading Scripture, and serving faithfully while secretly carrying assumptions such as:

- Nothing good ever happens to me.

• God blesses other people more than He blesses me.
• Things never work out for me.
• I probably shouldn't expect much.

These thoughts may seem harmless, but they create strongholds of unbelief that affect every area of life.

Biblical Examples of Unbelief

The Father of the Demon-Possessed Son

The father in Mark 9 gives one of the most honest prayers in Scripture. "Lord, I believe; help thou mine unbelief."

He acknowledged that faith and unbelief were operating at the same time. Many believers live there. They love God. They pray. They attend church. Yet they still have areas where unbelief remains. The first step in crushing unbelief is acknowledging it. You cannot conquer what you refuse to confront.

Israel in the Wilderness

God parted the Red Sea. God provided manna. God provided water. God defeated Pharaoh. Yet when they reached the Promised Land, they doubted. The issue was not God's ability. The issue was their belief. The giant they faced was not the Anakim. The giant was unbelief.

Saul of Tarsus

Before becoming the Apostle Paul, Saul was a man operating in unbelief concerning Jesus.

He had knowledge. He had religious training. He had passion. What he lacked was revelation. His unbelief caused him to fight the very thing God was doing.

Many people today possess information about God but lack revelation of God. Knowledge without revelation often produces unbelief.

The Two Mothers

Consider two mothers. Both need shoes for their sons. Both are praying. Both love God. Both have a legitimate need.

The first mother walks through an alley and finds one shoe. A little farther down she finds another shoe. The shoes happen to fit her son. She praises God because she believes God provided.

The second mother goes into Macy's. She walks through the store looking at shoes she cannot afford. A stranger approaches her. He purchases not only the shoes but clothes for her son as well. Then he gives her additional resources for herself.

Both mothers experienced provision. The question is not whether God provided. The question is which version of God do they believe? One mother believed God could barely meet the need. The other believed God could exceed the need. One expected survival. The other expected abundance. The difference was not God's ability. The difference was belief.

Many believers limit God not because God is limited, but because their expectations are limited. The greatest battle is often not receiving the promise. It is believing the promise is actually for us. Many people are not limited by God's power. They are limited by their picture of God.

The Clinical Perspective: Unbelief and Core Beliefs

From a cognitive behavioral therapy perspective, people operate from core beliefs. Core beliefs are deeply held assumptions about who I am, who others are, what the world is, and what God is like.

These beliefs become the lens through which every experience is interpreted.

For example:

- I am not worthy.
- Nothing good ever happens to me.

- People always leave.
- I never get a break.
- God helps everybody except me.

These beliefs become internal filters. Even when evidence exists that contradicts them, people unconsciously reject the evidence.

This is why two people can read the exact same Scripture and arrive at completely different expectations. One reads, "My God shall supply all your need." The other reads the same verse but secretly thinks, "Maybe for other people."

The issue is not the Scripture. The issue is the core belief.

Clinically, healing unbelief requires identifying the thought, challenging the thought, replacing the thought, and reinforcing the truth. Biblically, this is called renewing the mind.

Romans 12:2 tells us to be transformed by the renewing of our minds.

The Bible and cognitive behavioral therapy agree on one important principle:

Change the belief and you change the behavior.

What many believers call a faith problem is often a belief problem. Somewhere they have accepted a thought about themselves, their circumstances, or God that does not agree with Scripture. Until that belief is confronted, the cycle continues.

This is why crushing unbelief requires more than positive thinking. It requires transformation. It requires replacing every lie with truth until God's Word becomes more real than our experiences and His promises become more believable than our fears.

How to Crush the Giant of Unbelief

The first step is acknowledging it. The father in Mark 9 did not hide it. He admitted it. "Lord, I believe; help my unbelief." Many people cannot overcome unbelief because they refuse to admit it exists.

The second step is examining your picture of God. Your faith will never rise above your picture of God. Do you see Him as Provider? Healer? Deliverer? Rewarder? Father? Or do you secretly see Him as distant, reluctant, and hard to please?

The third step is renewing your mind through the Word of God. Many people read Scripture ritualistically rather than transformationally. Faith comes by hearing. Read the Word out loud. Meditate on it day and night. Personalize it. Speak it. Allow it to become part of your internal dialogue.

Ask God three questions:

• What do You want to say?
• What do You want to hear?
• What do You want to do?

These questions position you to receive instruction, strategy, direction, and revelation.

Finally, identify every belief that contradicts God's Word. Challenge it. Replace it. Reinforce the truth until the truth becomes stronger than the lie.

Signs You Are Battling Unbelief

- You expect disappointment.
- You struggle to imagine positive outcomes.
- You constantly focus on what could go wrong.
- You pray but secretly expect nothing to happen.
- You become uncomfortable when people talk about miracles.
- You minimize God's promises.
- You find reasons why Scripture will not work for you.
- You talk more about your problems than God's ability.

Prayer for Crushing Unbelief

Father, in the name of Jesus, I come before You acknowledging that there have been areas in my life where unbelief has been operating. Your Word declares that without faith it is impossible to please You, and today I ask You to expose every hidden place where I have agreed with fear, doubt, disappointment, limitation, and negative expectations more than I have agreed with Your promises.

Forgive me for every time I allowed my circumstances to become greater than my revelation of who You are. Forgive me for every time I trusted my past experiences more than I trusted Your Word. Forgive me for every time I allowed disappointment, delay, pain, rejection, loss, or unanswered questions to shape my view of You.

Father, I renounce every false belief that says You are unwilling to bless me, unwilling to provide for me, unwilling to heal me, unwilling to restore me, or unwilling to fulfill Your promises concerning my life. I reject every lie that has distorted my picture of You.

Your Word declares that You are Jehovah Jireh, my Provider. You are Jehovah Rapha, my Healer. You are El Shaddai, the All-Sufficient One. You are the God who is able to do exceedingly abundantly above all I can ask or think. Help me to see You as You truly are.

Lord, heal every wound that gave unbelief permission to enter my life. Heal every disappointment. Heal every betrayal. Heal every delay. Heal every place where my expectations were damaged. Restore my ability to trust You completely.

Renew my mind according to Your Word. Let every stronghold of unbelief be torn down. Let every limiting belief be broken. Let every negative expectation be replaced with faith-filled expectation. Teach me to trust Your character even when I do not understand Your timing.

I declare that my faith will not be governed by what I see, what I feel, or what I have experienced. My faith will be governed by what You have spoken.

I receive fresh faith, fresh vision, fresh expectation, and fresh confidence in You. I declare that the giant of unbelief is being crushed in my life. My confidence is returning. My hope is returning. My expectation is returning. My trust in You is being restored.

In Jesus' name, Amen.

Declarations for Crushing Unbelief

- I believe God is who He says He is.
- I believe God can do what He says He can do.
- I reject every lie that contradicts the Word of God.
- I will not allow my circumstances to define my expectations.
- My past disappointments will not dictate my future.
- I walk by faith and not by sight.
- I trust God's character even when I do not understand His process.
- I believe God is good.
- I believe God is faithful.
- I believe God is able.

• I believe God is willing.
• I believe God is working on my behalf.
• I believe every promise of God is yes and amen in Christ Jesus.
• I believe God is my Provider.
• I believe God is my Healer.
• I believe God is my Deliverer.
• I believe God is my Source.
• I believe God is opening doors that no man can shut.
• I believe God is making a way where there seems to be no way.
• I believe God is working all things together for my good.
• I reject the spirit of doubt.
• I reject the spirit of fear.
• I reject negative expectations.
• I reject limiting beliefs.
• I reject every thought that exalts itself against the knowledge of God.
• My mind is being renewed by the Word of God.
• My faith is increasing daily.
• My expectation is increasing daily.
• My confidence in God is increasing daily.
• I expect favor.
• I expect provision.
• I expect healing.

- I expect restoration.
- I expect breakthrough.
- I expect wisdom.
- I expect divine opportunities.
- I expect God to exceed my expectations.
- I will no longer agree with my circumstances over God's promises.
- I will no longer allow disappointment to shape my theology.
- I will no longer allow fear to limit my obedience.
- I choose to believe God.
- I choose to trust God.
- I choose to obey God.
- The giant of unbelief is being crushed.
- My faith is stronger than my fear.
- My expectation is stronger than my doubt.
- My confidence is stronger than my circumstances.
- I serve a God who is able to do exceedingly abundantly above all I ask or think.
- I am growing in faith.
- I am growing in trust.
- I am growing in expectation.
- I am growing in revelation.

• I believe God, and because I believe God, I will see the goodness of the Lord in the land of the living.

In Jesus' name, Amen.

ANXIETY

Meet the Giant

Anxiety is one of the most common giants people face today. In many ways, it has become the signature giant of modern culture. People are more connected than ever through technology, yet many have never felt more overwhelmed, fearful, exhausted, and uncertain.

Anxiety does not always arrive as panic attacks or emotional breakdowns. Sometimes it appears as overthinking. Sometimes it appears as sleepless nights. Sometimes it shows up as irritability, perfectionism, people pleasing, procrastination, indecisiveness, or the inability to relax. Sometimes it disguises itself as productivity. Other times it hides behind busyness. Many people who appear calm on the outside are fighting tremendous anxiety on the inside.

Anxiety is the constant anticipation that something bad is about to happen. It is the feeling that you must prepare for every possible disaster, solve every possible problem, and control every possible outcome.

The giant of anxiety whispers, "What if it doesn't work? What if something goes wrong? What if they leave? What if you fail? What if God doesn't come through?"

The challenge with anxiety is that it often disguises itself as wisdom. People think they are being responsible when they are actually worrying. They think they are preparing when they are actually obsessing. They think they are being cautious when they are actually being controlled by fear.

Anxiety keeps the mind living in a future that has not happened while preventing a person from fully living in the present that God has given them.

Jesus addressed anxiety directly because He knew it would become one of humanity's greatest struggles. In Matthew 6:34 He said, "Take therefore no thought for the morrow: for the morrow shall take thought for the things of itself."

Anxiety attempts to make you carry tomorrow's burdens with today's strength. The problem is that God only gives grace for today. When you try to carry tomorrow today, the weight becomes crushing.

One of the reasons anxiety is such a dangerous giant is because it rarely fights alone. Anxiety often travels with fear, rejection, trauma, grief, unbelief, perfectionism, and control. In many cases, anxiety is not the giant itself. It is the alarm system announcing that another giant is present.

What Is Anxiety Clinically?

From a clinical perspective, anxiety is characterized by excessive worry, nervousness, fear, apprehension, and heightened physical arousal. Anxiety disorders are among the most common mental health conditions worldwide.

Symptoms may include excessive worry, racing thoughts, restlessness, difficulty concentrating, muscle tension, irritability, sleep disturbances, increased heart rate, sweating, panic attacks, difficulty making decisions, avoidance behaviors, and a constant sense of dread or uneasiness.

Clinically, anxiety often develops when the brain perceives a threat. The body's fight, flight, or freeze response becomes activated. Adrenaline is released. Stress hormones increase. The body prepares to protect itself.

The challenge is that the brain often responds to perceived threats the same way it responds to real threats. A person may be physically safe while their nervous system acts as though danger is present.

Anxiety is not always a lack of faith. Sometimes it is a nervous system that has been overwhelmed. Sometimes it is trauma that has not been healed. Sometimes it is chronic stress. Sometimes it is unresolved grief. Sometimes it is learned behavior from childhood. Sometimes it develops from years of living in unpredictable environments where the brain learned to remain on constant alert.

This is why both spiritual healing and practical strategies are necessary. The goal is not simply to pray more. The goal is to allow God to heal the spirit, renew the mind, and regulate the body.

Signs You May Be Dealing with Anxiety

Many people are battling anxiety without realizing it. They assume their symptoms are simply part of their personality.

You may be dealing with anxiety if:

- You constantly imagine worst case scenarios.
- You struggle to relax even when nothing is wrong.
- You replay conversations repeatedly.
- You seek excessive reassurance from others.
- You have difficulty making decisions because you fear making the wrong choice.
- You feel guilty when resting.
- You overprepare for situations.
- You experience chronic tension in your body.
- You have difficulty sleeping because your mind won't slow down.
- You avoid situations because of fear of failure or embarrassment.
- You constantly feel responsible for things outside your control.

• You find yourself expecting bad news even during good seasons.

Anxiety often convinces people that their worry is helping them. In reality, anxiety rarely solves problems. It simply rehearses them.

The Spiritual Root of Anxiety

At its core, anxiety is often connected to trust. Anxiety asks, “Can God really be trusted with this?”

The giant of anxiety causes people to place greater confidence in worst case scenarios than in God’s promises. Anxiety magnifies problems and minimizes God’s power. It causes people to rehearse disaster more than they rehearse scripture.

Philippians 4:6-7 says, “Be careful for nothing; but in every thing by prayer and supplication with thanksgiving let your requests be made known unto God.”

Notice Paul did not say ignore your concerns. He said bring them to God. Prayer is not pretending the problem does not exist. Prayer is transferring the burden to someone stronger than you.

The spiritual battle of anxiety is often a battle over trust, surrender, and control. Anxiety says, "I must control everything." Faith says,"God is in control."

Anxiety in the Bible

The Bible is full of people who battled anxiety.

Elijah

After one of the greatest victories of his life on Mount Carmel, Elijah became overwhelmed. One threat from Jezebel sent him running into the wilderness. He became exhausted, discouraged, fearful, and emotionally depleted.

Notice God's response. God did not immediately rebuke him. God fed him. God allowed him to rest. God restored him. Sometimes the most spiritual thing a person can do is sleep.

Exhaustion often amplifies anxiety. A tired mind will often interpret situations more negatively than a rested one.

Martha

Luke 10:41 says, "Martha, Martha, thou art careful and troubled about many things."

The word careful means anxious. Martha was serving Jesus while simultaneously being anxious.

This reveals an important truth. People can be busy for God while being anxious. Activity is not always peace. Busyness is not always faith. Sometimes people stay busy because slowing down would force them to confront what is happening inside them.

The Disciples in the Storm

Mark 4 records the disciples panicking during a storm while Jesus slept. The storm was real. The danger felt real. Yet Jesus was resting.

The difference between Jesus and the disciples was not the presence of the storm. It was the perspective of the storm. Faith sees the storm through God's promises. Anxiety sees God's promises through the storm.

Anxiety and Trauma

Many anxious people are not simply worrying. They are protecting themselves.

Trauma teaches the brain, "Something bad happened before, so something bad could happen again." The brain becomes hypervigilant. Hypervigilance keeps people scanning for danger. It is exhausting.

Trauma survivors often become experts at anticipating problems because anticipation once helped them survive. The problem is that survival mode is difficult to turn off. This is why healing trauma often reduces anxiety. The giant of anxiety frequently sits on top of unresolved wounds.

What Anxiety Looks Like in Leaders

Anxiety attacks leaders because leaders carry responsibility. Leaders often feel responsible for outcomes they cannot control. They carry vision, people, finances, decisions, conflicts, expectations, deadlines, and organizational pressures.

The giant whispers, "What if the ministry fails? What if the people leave? What if the finances run out? What if you make the wrong decision? What if you are exposed as not being enough?"

Anxious leaders often overwork, micromanage, struggle to delegate, feel guilty when resting, fear disappointing people, constantly second guess themselves, and attempt to control every detail.

Many leaders become addicted to activity because activity temporarily distracts them from anxiety.

Anxiety often attacks leaders through responsibility overload. The enemy knows that if he can exhaust a leader mentally, he can weaken an entire vision.

Many leadership problems are not character problems. They are anxiety problems. A leader who cannot rest will eventually become ineffective. A leader who cannot trust God will eventually attempt to become God in every situation by controlling everything around them.

What Anxiety Looks Like in Creatives

Creatives are particularly vulnerable to anxiety because creatives live in possibility. Their minds naturally generate ideas, scenarios, solutions, visions, and alternatives. The same imagination that creates innovation can also create anxiety.

Creatives often battle perfectionism, fear of criticism, fear of failure, comparison, imposter syndrome, starting projects but not finishing them, and analysis paralysis.

The giant tells creatives, "What if it's not good enough? What if nobody likes it? What if someone else does it better? What if you fail publicly? What if you create something and no one responds?"

The giant of anxiety has buried countless books, songs, businesses, ministries, inventions, sermons, paintings, and creative projects. Not because people lacked talent, but because they lacked peace.

Anxiety often attacks creatives through comparison. It causes them to compare their beginning to someone else's middle. It causes them to compare their behind the scenes struggles to someone else's highlight reel.

Anxiety also attacks creatives through perfectionism. The creative becomes so concerned about creating something perfect that they never finish anything at all. Many creative dreams are not destroyed by failure. They are destroyed by fear of failure.

How to Crush the Giant of Anxiety

Identify the Underlying Fear

Anxiety is often a symptom. Ask yourself, "What am I afraid will happen?" Most anxiety has a specific fear underneath it. Find the fear. Challenge the fear. Replace the fear.

Renew Your Thinking

Romans 12:2 teaches transformation through renewed thinking. Clinically, this aligns with Cognitive Behavioral Therapy. CBT teaches that thoughts influence emotions.

Many anxious thoughts are cognitive distortions including catastrophizing, fortune telling, mind reading, and worst-case thinking.

Challenge the thought.

Ask yourself:

Is this fact or fear? Is there evidence for this belief? What would I tell someone else in this situation? What does God say?

Practice Present Moment Awareness

Anxiety lives in the future. Peace lives in the present.

Ask yourself:

Where are my feet right now? What is actually happening right now? What has God provided today?

Jesus repeatedly brought people back to today.

Develop Healthy Rhythms

Sleep. Exercise. Nutrition. Rest. Boundaries. These are not merely physical disciplines. They are spiritual disciplines. A depleted body often produces an anxious mind.

Pray Specifically

General worries require specific prayers. Name the concern. Release the concern. Trust God with the concern. Prayer is not informing God. Prayer is surrendering control.

Replace Worry with Worship

Worry magnifies problems. Worship magnifies God. You cannot simultaneously magnify God's greatness and the giant's size. One will always become larger than the other.

Build Community

Anxiety grows in isolation. Healing grows in connection. Talk to trusted people. Seek wise counsel. Consider professional counseling when needed. God often sends healing through people.

Key Scriptures for Crushing Anxiety

Philippians 4:6-7, Isaiah 41:10, 2 Timothy 1:7, 1 Peter 5:7, Matthew 6:25-34, Psalm 55:22, Joshua 1:9, John 14:27, Psalm 94:19, Isaiah 26:3

Giant-Killing Truths

• Anxiety predicts problems; faith trusts God.
• Anxiety demands certainty; faith requires trust.
• Anxiety focuses on what might happen; faith focuses on who God is.

• Anxiety magnifies danger; faith magnifies God.
• Anxiety lives in tomorrow; peace lives in today.
• You do not have to carry what God never asked you to carry.
• The same God who brought you this far will carry you the rest of the way.

Anxiety is often the bridge between fear and unbelief. Fear says, "Something bad could happen." Anxiety spends all day rehearsing it. Unbelief eventually concludes, "God probably will not help me."

That progression makes anxiety one of the most strategic giants to crush. If you can stop anxiety from taking root, you can often prevent fear from becoming unbelief and worry from becoming a stronghold.

Prayer for Crushing Anxiety

Father, in the name of Jesus, I surrender every anxious thought, every fear, every burden, and every concern to You. Forgive me for carrying what belongs in Your hands. Teach me to trust You completely.

I cast my cares upon You because You care for me. Heal every wound, every trauma, every disappointment, and every fear that has contributed to anxiety in my life.

Renew my mind. Strengthen my faith. Quiet every storm within me. Let Your peace guard my heart and mind through Christ Jesus.

I declare that anxiety will not control my decisions, my relationships, my calling, or my future.

I choose faith over fear. I choose peace over panic. I choose trust over worry.

In Jesus' name,

Amen.

Declarations for Crushing Anxiety

• I have not been given a spirit of fear but of power, love, and a sound mind.
• My mind belongs to Christ.
• I will not be controlled by anxiety.
• God's peace guards my heart and mind.
• I trust God with my future.
• I trust God with my family.
• I trust God with my finances.
• I trust God with my calling.
• I trust God with the things I cannot control.
• My peace is greater than my panic.
• My faith is greater than my fear.
• Every giant of anxiety must fall in Jesus' name.
• I am not merely defeating anxiety. I am crushing it.

LONELINESS

The Silent Giant That Convinces You That You Are Alone

Scriptures

"Turn to me and be gracious to me, for I am lonely and afflicted." — Psalm 25:16

"I will never leave you nor forsake you." — Hebrews 13:5

"Two are better than one." — Ecclesiastes 4:9-10

GIANT PROFILE

Name: Loneliness

Alias: Isolation, Disconnection, Abandonment, Emotional Separation

Favorite Weapon: Isolation

Favorite Attack: Convincing people that nobody understands, nobody cares, and nobody is coming.

Goal: To separate you from God, healthy relationships, purpose, and community.

What It Says:

- Nobody cares about you.
- You are all by yourself.
- Nobody understands what you're going through.
- You don't belong.
- You are forgotten.
- You might as well withdraw.

Weakness:

Connection, vulnerability, community, truth, and the presence of God.

THE GIANT'S DEFINITION

Loneliness is more than being alone. Being alone is a physical condition, but loneliness is an emotional and spiritual condition. You can be alone and not be lonely. You can also be surrounded by people and still feel completely alone.

Loneliness is the painful feeling that you are disconnected from meaningful relationships, unseen by others, and unsupported in life's struggles. The Giant of Loneliness thrives when people begin withdrawing from others, stop sharing their struggles, and convince themselves that isolation is safer than connection.

What makes this giant so dangerous is that it often hides in plain sight. Many people smile publicly while suffering privately. Many lead ministries while battling loneliness. Many sit in churches every Sunday feeling unseen. Many are active on social media but disconnected in real life.

Loneliness does not always look like isolation. Sometimes it looks like performance. Sometimes it looks like busyness. Sometimes it looks like achievement. Sometimes it looks like success. Yet underneath it all, the heart quietly cries out for connection.

THE REALITY OF LONELINESS

Loneliness has become so widespread that health experts now consider it a public health crisis.

In 2023, the United States Surgeon General issued an advisory warning about the epidemic of loneliness and social isolation in America. Research cited in that advisory found that lacking social connection can increase the risk of premature death at levels comparable to smoking up to fifteen cigarettes per day. The report also linked chronic loneliness to increased risks of anxiety, depression, heart disease, dementia, stroke, and other serious health challenges.

One survey found that seventy-six percent of older adults identified Sunday as the loneliest day of the week.

Think about that for a moment.

The very day that was designed for worship, rest, fellowship, and family has become one of the hardest days for many people.

Why?

Because Sunday often magnifies whatever is missing. If family is absent, you feel it. If relationships are broken, you feel it. If community is lacking, you feel it. If grief is present, you feel it.

The Giant of Loneliness often becomes loudest when everything around you becomes quiet.

ROOTS OF THE GIANT

Loneliness often develops through rejection, abandonment, grief and loss, trauma, church hurt, divorce, betrayal, relocation, depression, fear of vulnerability, and unhealed emotional wounds.

Sometimes loneliness is caused by what happened to you. Other times it is caused by what happened in you.

After enough disappointment, people often build walls around their hearts. The problem is that walls that keep pain out also keep people out. Eventually protection becomes isolation, and isolation becomes loneliness.

BIBLICAL EXAMPLES

Elijah

After one of the greatest victories of his life, Elijah found himself isolated, exhausted, and discouraged. He told God, “I alone am left” (1 Kings 19).

Yet Elijah’s perception was not reality. God revealed that thousands remained faithful. Loneliness distorted Elijah’s vision. The giant convinced him he was alone when he was not.

David

David frequently wrote about seasons of loneliness. He experienced rejection from family, was hunted by Saul, separated from friends, and forced to live in caves.

Yet David continually returned to God’s presence. Instead of allowing loneliness to drive him away from God, he allowed it to drive him toward God.

Jesus

Even Jesus experienced loneliness.

His closest disciples fell asleep during His greatest moment of agony. Peter denied Him. Judas betrayed Him. The crowd abandoned Him.

Yet Jesus remained connected to the Father. His example teaches us that loneliness may visit us, but it does not have to define us.

SIGNS YOU ARE DEALING WITH THIS GIANT

You may be battling the Giant of Loneliness if you withdraw from people when you are hurting, feel unseen or unimportant, struggle to trust others, feel disconnected even in groups, avoid vulnerability, convince yourself that nobody understands, spend excessive time isolated, secretly feel forgotten, battle sadness after social interactions, or believe that asking for help is weakness.

Many people do not recognize loneliness because they assume loneliness only exists when someone has no one around them. However, some of the loneliest people in the world are surrounded by crowds. The issue is not always proximity to people. Often it is the absence of genuine connection.

HOW THIS GIANT OPERATES IN LEADERSHIP

Leadership can be one of the loneliest places in the world. Leaders are often surrounded by people but lack genuine connection.

Many leaders have people who need them but very few people who truly know them. The Giant of Loneliness attacks leaders by convincing them they must carry everything alone.

It whispers, “You can’t tell anyone. You have to be strong all the time. Nobody will understand. People need your answers, not your honesty."

Eventually leaders stop receiving support while continually giving support. When that happens, burnout becomes a real possibility.

Healthy leaders build healthy relationships. Healthy leaders seek counsel. Healthy leaders remain connected.

HOW THIS GIANT OPERATES IN CREATIVES

Creatives often experience loneliness differently.

Because they see deeply, feel deeply, and process deeply, they can sometimes feel misunderstood. The Giant of Loneliness attacks creatives by convincing them that nobody understands their vision, their purpose, or their journey.

Many creatives become isolated because they fear rejection. Others withdraw because repeated disappointment has made connection feel risky.

But creativity flourishes in healthy community. The gift grows stronger when connected to the right people. Isolation suffocates creativity. Connection strengthens it.

HOW TO CRUSH THE GIANT OF LONELINESS

Reject the Lie That You Are Alone

Loneliness may be a feeling, but it is not a fact. God's presence remains even when His presence is not felt. Feelings change. Truth remains.

Move Toward Connection

The giant wants isolation. Do the opposite. Call someone. Attend the gathering. Join the group. Show up. Connection rarely happens accidentally. It often happens intentionally.

Become Vulnerable

Healing begins where honesty starts. You cannot be fully known if you never allow people to know you. Safe vulnerability destroys isolation.

Build Kingdom Community

Ecclesiastes teaches us that two are better than one. God never intended for believers to walk alone. Find people who challenge you, encourage you, and strengthen your faith.

Strengthen Your Relationship With God

Human connection is important. But no human relationship can completely fill a God-shaped space. The deepest answer to loneliness is intimacy with God.

The Giant of Loneliness is ultimately defeated when we learn that God's presence is not merely a theological concept but a daily reality. The enemy wants you disconnected because disconnected people become vulnerable to discouragement, deception, depression, and despair. However, when you remain connected to God and connected to healthy community, loneliness begins to lose its power.

PRAYER TO CRUSH THE GIANT OF LONELINESS

Father, in the name of Jesus, I come before You acknowledging every place where loneliness has attempted to take root in my life.

I renounce the lies that tell me I am forgotten, abandoned, unseen, or unloved. Your Word declares that You will never leave me nor forsake me, and today I choose to believe Your truth over my feelings.

Heal every wound created by rejection, abandonment, betrayal, disappointment, and loss. Restore my ability to trust again. Give me the courage to reach out instead of withdrawing.

Bring healthy relationships into my life and remove every unhealthy pattern that keeps me isolated.

Surround me with people who will encourage my faith, strengthen my purpose, and help me walk in destiny.

Where loneliness has produced sadness, release joy. Where isolation has produced fear, release peace. Where separation has produced pain, release healing.

Teach me to find my deepest security in Your presence.

I declare that I am not alone. I am loved. I am seen. I am known. I am connected.

And by the power of Jesus Christ, I crush the Giant of Loneliness.

Amen.

GIANT-CRUSHING DECLARATIONS

- I am never alone because God is with me.
- I reject every lie of abandonment and rejection.

- I am loved, valued, and connected.
- I will not isolate myself from healthy relationships.
- I choose connection over withdrawal.
- I choose vulnerability over fear.
- I choose community over isolation.
- I refuse to allow loneliness to define my identity.
- God is surrounding me with the right people.
- My relationships will flourish.
- My heart will heal.
- My joy will return.
- My purpose will thrive.
- I am not abandoned.
- I am not forgotten.
- I am not invisible.
- I am a Giant Crusher.
- And I have crushed the Giant of Loneliness.

REBELLION

Introduction

Rebellion is one of the most destructive giants a believer can face because it often disguises itself as independence, strength, individuality, or personal conviction. Unlike many giants that attack from the outside, rebellion often develops within the heart. It begins when a person resists correction, rejects authority, refuses instruction, or insists on their own way regardless of God's direction.

At its core, rebellion is not merely disagreement. It is resistance against rightful authority.

The danger of rebellion is that it blinds the individual to the very thing that is destroying them. A rebellious person often believes they are fighting for freedom when in reality they are becoming enslaved to pride, self-will, offense, and deception.

Many people who struggle with rebellion are gifted. They are intelligent, creative, visionary, and capable leaders. Yet gifts cannot protect a person from the consequences of rebellion. In fact, rebellion has destroyed more callings than weakness ever has. The enemy understands that if he can disconnect a believer from accountability, correction, and submission to God, he can eventually disconnect them from purpose.

Rebellion is not simply a behavioral issue. It is a spiritual giant. And it must be crushed.

What Is Rebellion?

Biblically, rebellion is the refusal to submit to God's authority, God's order, God's instruction, or God-appointed leadership. It is choosing self-will over God's will.

Rebellion says, "I know what God said, but I want to do what I want."

It is the attitude that elevates personal desires above divine instruction.

The first rebellion in Scripture occurred in heaven when Satan refused to remain in his assigned position and attempted to exalt himself above God.

Isaiah 14:13-14 says, "You said in your heart, 'I will ascend into heaven; I will exalt my throne above the stars of God.'"

Before Satan became an adversary, he became rebellious.

Every major rebellion in Scripture follows a similar pattern. Pride leads to rebellion. Rebellion leads to deception. Deception leads to destruction. What begins as resistance eventually becomes separation. What begins as self-will eventually becomes self-deception. Every act of rebellion carries consequences because rebellion places human desire above divine wisdom.

The Clinical Perspective

From a clinical standpoint, rebellion can sometimes manifest through what behavioral specialists call oppositional behaviors, authority resistance, defiance patterns, or maladaptive responses to control and trauma.

While rebellion is primarily a spiritual issue in Scripture, some individuals develop rebellious tendencies because of unhealed wounds, abuse, broken trust, authoritarian environments, rejection, neglect, and control-based relationships.

Many people who appear rebellious are actually wounded. Their resistance developed as a defense mechanism. The problem is that what may have once protected them can later hinder them. A person may learn to distrust authority because authority previously hurt them. Unfortunately, that distrust can eventually extend toward spiritual authority, healthy relationships, mentors, leaders, and even God Himself.

Healing the wound does not excuse rebellion, but it often helps explain its origin. Understanding where rebellion began is often the first step toward breaking its power.

The Root of Rebellion

Most rebellion grows from several roots:

- Pride
- Offense
- Bitterness
- Unforgiveness
- Independence
- Distrust
- Control
- Self-will
- Fear of vulnerability

The rebellious heart often says, “No one can tell me what to do.” It says, “I already know.” It says, “I don’t need accountability.” It says, “I don’t need correction.”

The moment correction becomes an enemy instead of a gift, rebellion has begun to grow.

Many people do not recognize rebellion because they assume rebellion is always loud, aggressive, and obvious. In reality, rebellion can be quiet. It can hide behind excuses, rationalizations, and justifications. It can wear the mask of intelligence, gifting, experience, or even spirituality. Yet beneath the surface is a heart that resists yielding to God.

Why God Hates Rebellion

God opposes rebellion because rebellion attacks divine order.

Everything God created operates through order. The universe functions through order. Families function through order. The church functions through order. Leadership functions through order. Kingdom advancement functions through order.

Rebellion creates disorder.

Where rebellion is present, confusion soon follows. Where confusion exists, division eventually appears. Where division appears, progress becomes difficult. Rebellion tears apart what order is attempting to build.

God is not opposed to creativity, innovation, or growth. He is opposed to chaos. Rebellion creates chaos because it refuses alignment with divine structure.

Rebellion Is As the Sin of Witchcraft

Scripture

1 Samuel 15:23 says, "For rebellion is as the sin of witchcraft, and stubbornness is as iniquity and idolatry."

This is one of the strongest statements in Scripture concerning rebellion. Notice God did not say rebellion is witchcraft. He said rebellion is as the sin of witchcraft. Why? Because both rebellion and witchcraft seek control outside of God's authority.

Witchcraft operates through manipulation, control, domination, intimidation, coercion, fear, and counterfeit authority. Witchcraft seeks to influence people without submission to God. Rebellion seeks independence from God. Both reject divine authority.

This is why rebellion often partners with manipulation. A rebellious person may refuse authority over themselves while simultaneously attempting to control others. The spirit behind rebellion wants power without accountability. It wants influence without submission. It wants authority without surrender.

Throughout Scripture, witchcraft is not merely about spells or occult practices. At its core, it is an attempt to control outcomes, people, situations, and environments apart from God's authority and methods. Whenever manipulation becomes the preferred method over trust and obedience, the spirit of rebellion is often present.

Biblical Examples of Rebellion

Lucifer

Lucifer rebelled against God. His pride convinced him he deserved more than what God assigned him. His rebellion cost him heaven.

Many people lose their assignment because they become dissatisfied with their position. Rather than being faithful where they are, they become consumed with where they wish they were. Lucifer reminds us that pride often precedes rebellion.

Adam and Eve

God gave one instruction. The serpent introduced an alternative. Their rebellion opened the door to sin, separation, and suffering.

Every act of rebellion ultimately produces consequences beyond the individual. Adam and Eve's decision affected generations. Rebellion never remains isolated. It always impacts someone else.

Korah

Korah challenged the authority of Moses. His rebellion appeared spiritual. He argued that everyone was holy. However, his true issue was ambition. He wanted authority he had not been assigned. His rebellion led to destruction.

Many modern rebellions begin the same way. People confuse calling with entitlement. They assume that being gifted automatically qualifies them for positions that God has not yet assigned or prepared them for.

King Saul

Saul partially obeyed God. Partial obedience is still disobedience. Saul's rebellion cost him the kingdom.

Many believers want God's blessings while reserving the right to ignore God's instructions. Saul teaches us that rebellion can coexist with religious activity. A person can appear spiritual while remaining rebellious. They can worship publicly while resisting God privately.

Absalom

Absalom rebelled against his father David. He won people's hearts through charm, influence, and political manipulation. He built a following before attempting to seize the throne.

Absalom demonstrates how rebellion often spreads through offense. Offended people gather offended people. Unhealed wounds become breeding grounds for rebellion. What begins as hurt eventually becomes division when it is left unresolved.

Signs You Are Dealing With Rebellion

A rebellious giant may be operating when:

- You resist correction.

- You become defensive when confronted.
- You refuse accountability.
- You isolate yourself from wise counsel.
- You consistently blame others.
- You struggle with submission.
- You reject authority figures.
- You justify disobedience.
- You become easily offended.
- You insist on your own way.
- You view correction as rejection.
- You avoid people who challenge you.
- You secretly believe you know better than everyone else.

The purpose of this list is not condemnation but awareness. What is revealed can be healed. What is exposed can be addressed. What is acknowledged can be transformed.

What Rebellion Does

Rebellion Disconnects You from Wisdom

Proverbs 12:15 says, "The way of a fool is right in his own eyes: but he that hearkeneth unto counsel is wise."

Rebellion rejects counsel. Without counsel, mistakes multiply. Wisdom often enters through instruction, but rebellion closes the door that wisdom is trying to enter.

Rebellion Produces Isolation

The rebellious person eventually pushes away mentors, leaders, friends, and accountability partners. Isolation becomes fertile ground for deception because there is no one present to challenge faulty thinking.

Rebellion Delays Purpose

Many people are waiting for promotion while refusing the process required for promotion. Submission often precedes elevation. God frequently tests character before He releases greater responsibility.

Rebellion Opens Doors to Deception

When a person rejects truth, they become vulnerable to counterfeit truth. Deception thrives where rebellion exists. Once correction is rejected, deception becomes easier to accept.

Rebellion Creates Division

Rebellion rarely stays personal. It spreads. It affects families, teams, ministries, businesses, and organizations. One rebellious spirit can create confusion for an entire group.

Rebellion in Creatives

Creatives are often visionaries. They think differently. They see possibilities others miss. This is part of their gifting.

However, the very strengths that make creatives powerful can also make them vulnerable to rebellion.

Creatives often struggle with correction, structure, accountability, process, timing, and authority. Many creatives mistake accountability for limitation. They view guidance as restriction. They see structure as control.

Yet structure is often what protects the gift.

The enemy targets creatives because creatives shape environments. Environments influence atmosphere. Atmosphere influences culture. Culture influences people.

If the enemy can make creatives rebellious, he can influence entire environments. A rebellious creative can spread disorder through music, media, art, leadership, communication, and influence.

The most effective creatives learn submission without losing innovation. They discover that accountability does not diminish creativity; it strengthens it. The most powerful gifts are gifts that have been surrendered to God.

Rebellion in Leadership

Rebellion in leadership is especially dangerous because leaders influence others. A rebellious leader often becomes unteachable, defensive, controlling, independent, unaccountable, and correction-resistant.

Leaders who stop learning eventually stop growing. Many leadership failures begin long before the public collapse. They begin when leaders stop receiving correction.

The greatest leaders remain teachable. They understand that accountability is protection, not punishment. They recognize that no matter how high they rise, they still need people who can speak truth into their lives.

Leadership without accountability eventually becomes dangerous. Authority without humility often becomes destructive.

Rebellion in Ministry

In ministry, rebellion often disguises itself as spiritual maturity. People may say, "God told me." They may say, "I don't need leadership." They may say, "I answer only to God." They may say, "I have my own ministry."

While God absolutely speaks to individuals, He also works through order, counsel, accountability, and spiritual covering. Ministry rebellion often produces church splits, division, competition, offense, manipulation, and confusion.

The Kingdom advances through unity, not rebellion. One of the enemy's greatest strategies is to convince gifted people that accountability is unnecessary. The truth is that every gift needs guidance, every calling needs maturity, and every ministry needs humility.

How to Crush the Giant of Rebellion

Recognize It

You cannot conquer what you refuse to acknowledge. Ask God to reveal hidden rebellion. Invite the Holy Spirit to search your heart and expose areas where resistance has become normal.

Repent Quickly

Repentance restores alignment. The faster repentance occurs, the less damage rebellion creates. Repentance is not weakness. It is wisdom.

Embrace Correction

Correction is not rejection. Correction is protection. Wise people grow from correction. Foolish people run from it. Every correction is an opportunity to become better.

Heal the Wounds

Many rebellious patterns began with pain. Allow God to heal the roots. A healed heart responds differently than a wounded heart.

Develop Accountability

Everyone needs someone who can challenge them. Accountability protects purpose. It provides perspective when emotions become clouded and helps keep us aligned with truth.

Choose Submission Daily

Submission is not weakness. Submission is strength under control. Submission is not about losing your voice. It is about aligning your voice with God's will.

Follow Christ's Example

Philippians 2:8 says, "And being found in fashion as a man, he humbled himself, and became obedient unto death."

Jesus conquered through obedience. We crush rebellion the same way. Every act of obedience weakens rebellion. Every surrendered decision strengthens spiritual maturity. Every humble response diminishes the power of self-will.

Prayer to Crush Rebellion

Father, in the name of Jesus, I repent for every area of rebellion, pride, stubbornness, self-will, resistance, and disobedience. Reveal every hidden place where I have resisted Your voice, rejected correction, or elevated my own opinion above Your truth. Remove every root of offense, bitterness, pride, fear, and distrust that has produced rebellion in my life.

Heal every wound that caused me to resist healthy authority. Give me a teachable spirit, a humble heart, and ears that hear Your instruction. Deliver me from manipulation, control, stubbornness, and self-deception. Help me walk in obedience, submission, wisdom, and maturity.

Align my heart with Your will and Your purpose. Let every rebellious stronghold be broken and every area of my life come into divine order. In Jesus' name, Amen.

Declarations for Crushing Rebellion

- I renounce rebellion, pride, stubbornness, and self-will.
- I choose obedience over resistance.
- I choose submission over pride.
- I choose wisdom over self-deception.
- I receive correction as protection.
- I am teachable, humble, and accountable.
- I honor wise counsel.
- My wounds will not dictate my responses.
- I will not allow offense to control my decisions.
- I walk in divine order.
- I submit my thoughts, desires, plans, and actions to God.

- I reject manipulation, control, intimidation, and witchcraft.
- I walk in the Spirit and not in the flesh.
- I honor God-appointed authority.
- I am aligned with God's purpose for my life.
- I crush the giant of rebellion and walk in obedience, freedom, humility, and victory.

Victory is not merely resisting rebellion once. Victory is developing a lifestyle of obedience. A defeated giant may fall for a season, but a crushed giant cannot rise in the same form. When rebellion is crushed, obedience becomes strength, humility becomes protection, and purpose can move forward unhindered.

OFFENSE

THE GIANT OF Bitterness, Division, Emotional Toxicity, and Spiritual Blindmess

Scripture Focus

Luke 17:1, Proverbs 19:11, Hebrews 12:15, Matthew 24:10, Proverbs 18:19, Ephesians 4:31–32, Proverbs 4:23

Meaning

Offense is more than hurt feelings. Offense is a spiritual trap. It is one of the enemy's most subtle and destructive weapons because it poisons the heart while convincing the individual that they are justified in their pain, attitude, and behavior. Offense causes isolation, pride, division, and spiritual blindness. It slowly alters perception until a person can no longer clearly distinguish between conviction and attack, correction and rejection, accountability and dishonor.

One of the most dangerous parts of offense is that many offended believers genuinely believe they are spiritually right while being emotionally toxic. They often become blind to their own bitterness because offense disguises itself as discernment, wisdom, or righteousness. The offended person begins filtering everything through pain. They hear correction as control. They hear truth as disrespect. They hear accountability as persecution. Offense hardens the heart and distorts spiritual vision.

So many people today are deeply offended. Offended by leadership. Offended by truth. Offended by correction. Offended because they were not celebrated. Offended because they were overlooked. Offended because someone challenged their behavior, questioned their motives, or exposed areas that still needed healing. Many believers continue functioning publicly while privately carrying deep offense in their hearts. They worship offended. They serve offended. They lead offended. They preach offended. Yet offense left unresolved eventually contaminates relationships, churches, families, leadership, creativity, and spiritual growth.

Offense is not harmless. It is not "just how I feel." It is a giant designed to poison the heart, divide people, destroy unity, and disconnect believers from healing, maturity, and freedom.

Context

The word "offense" in Scripture often refers to a stumbling block, snare, or trap. Jesus Himself said in Luke 17:1, "It is impossible but that offences will come." In other words, opportunities to become offended are unavoidable in life. The issue is not whether offense will come. The issue is whether you will allow it to take root within your spirit.

The enemy understands that if he cannot destroy you externally, he will attempt to poison you internally. He knows that bitterness can destroy a person from the inside long before visible destruction appears on the outside. Many people who are no longer struggling with outward sin are still bound internally by resentment, offense, jealousy, bitterness, and unresolved wounds.

An offended heart becomes vulnerable to division, suspicion, and isolation. Offense changes how people interpret conversations, relationships, leadership, and even the voice of God. What was once received as wisdom now feels offensive. What once brought growth now feels like attack. Offense causes people to disconnect from the very people God may have sent to help heal, strengthen, sharpen, or mature them.

The enemy uses offense because offended people often sabotage themselves while believing they are protecting themselves.

Roots of Offense

Offense often grows from rejection, pride, insecurity, jealousy, trauma, comparison, betrayal, disappointment, unhealed wounds, unmet expectations, and unresolved pain. Many people are not reacting only to the present situation. They are reacting from wounds that were never properly healed.

Sometimes a small disagreement triggers a massive emotional response because the offense is connected to years of buried hurt. What appears to be anger toward one moment may actually be pain from many moments compounded together. Some people are offended because they never healed from abandonment. Others are offended because pride refuses correction. Others are offended because insecurity interprets everything personally.

Unhealed wounds create hypersensitive reactions. Pain that is not healed eventually becomes pain that controls perception.

Offense also grows where humility is absent. Proverbs 19:11 says, "The discretion of a man deferreth his anger; and it is his glory to pass over a transgression." Mature people do not magnify every disagreement, every misunderstanding, or every disappointment. Wisdom teaches restraint, patience, and emotional maturity. Pride, however, feeds offense because pride constantly demands validation, recognition, apology, and vindication.

How This Giants Operates

OFFENSE DISTORTS PERCEPTION

An offended person begins interpreting life through wounded emotions. Suspicion increases. Defensiveness increases. Assumptions increase. They begin hearing conversations through pain instead of clarity. Eventually they become hypersensitive, easily triggered, and emotionally reactive. The danger is that offense convinces people their distorted perception is actually discernment.

OFFENSE CREATES ISOLATION

Offense often pushes people into emotional withdrawal and isolation. People stop communicating. They disconnect from healthy relationships. They avoid accountability. They pull away from community while convincing themselves they are protecting their peace. In reality, isolation often deepens the wound instead of healing it.

The enemy loves isolated believers because isolation weakens perspective, wisdom, accountability, and emotional health.

OFFENSE PRODUCES PRIDE

Pride keeps offense alive. Pride refuses to forgive. Pride refuses to heal. Pride constantly rehearses the wound and demands repayment for pain. Pride says, "I will never let this go." But humility creates room for healing, forgiveness, growth, and restoration.

Many people stay emotionally stuck because pride has partnered with offense.

OFFENSE CREATES DIVISION

Matthew 24:10 says, "And then shall many be offended, and shall betray one another, and shall hate one another." Notice the progression. Offense leads to betrayal. Betrayal leads to hatred. Many broken relationships began with unresolved offense. Many divided churches began with offense. Many damaged ministries began with offense. Many fractured families began with offense that was never confronted properly.

Offense divides what God intended to unite.

OFFENSE PRODUCES SPIRITUAL BLINDNESS

Hebrews 12:15 warns us about the "root of bitterness." Bitterness blinds discernment and contaminates relationships. Offended people often cannot clearly see their own behavior because pain has distorted perspective. They may continue ministering publicly while privately becoming bitter, cynical, prideful, angry, and emotionally unhealthy.

Spiritual blindness is dangerous because eventually people begin defending unhealthy behavior while believing they are spiritually justified.

Biblical Examples of Offense

CAIN

Cain became offended when God accepted Abel's sacrifice but rejected his. Instead of humbling himself and correcting his heart, Cain allowed offense to grow into jealousy, anger, and eventually murder. God warned him that sin was lying at the door, but Cain nurtured offense instead of crushing it. Offense eventually transformed into destruction.

SAUL

Saul became offended by David's success, favor, and recognition. The women celebrated David's victories, and Saul internalized their words through insecurity and pride. His offense turned into jealousy, obsession, paranoia, and rage. Saul spent more time chasing David than fulfilling his assignment as king. Offense distracted him from purpose and eventually contributed to his downfall.

THE OLDER BROTHER

In Luke 15, the older brother became offended by the father's grace toward the prodigal son. Instead of celebrating restoration, he isolated himself outside the celebration. Offense made him resent mercy. Many people cannot celebrate others because bitterness has poisoned their hearts.

JONAH

Jonah became offended because God showed mercy to Nineveh. He was angry that God forgave people he believed deserved judgment. His offense caused him to value his emotions more than God's compassion. Offense often causes people to prioritize personal feelings above God's heart.

THE PHARISEES

The Pharisees were constantly offended by Jesus because truth exposed their pride, hypocrisy, and traditions. They were offended by correction, offended by conviction, and offended by truth itself. Their offense blinded them so deeply that they rejected the very Messiah sent to save them.

Signs You Are Dealing With Offense

Constant irritation, defensiveness, bitterness, passive aggression, withdrawal, unforgiveness, jealousy, hypersensitivity, emotional reactivity, repeated replaying of conversations, suspicion, difficulty receiving correction, celebrating others' failures, refusing reconciliation, constantly feeling attacked, and emotional toxicity disguised as spirituality are all signs that offense may be operating in your heart.

One of the most dangerous places to be spiritually is emotionally wounded while fully convinced you are right.

Offense in Leadership and Ministry

Offense destroys many leaders privately before failure ever appears publicly. Offended leaders often become defensive, suspicious, controlling, emotionally reactive, prideful, isolated, and difficult to correct. When leaders internalize criticism improperly, offense can slowly transform into bitterness and emotional toxicity.

Many ministries have been damaged because leaders carried unresolved wounds. Offended leaders sometimes compete instead of collaborate. They become threatened by others' growth, influence, or success. They may secretly celebrate another leader's failure because offense has distorted their heart.

Healthy leaders remain teachable. Healthy leaders heal. Healthy leaders stay accountable. Healthy leaders refuse to allow bitterness to poison their assignment.

Offense and Creatives

Creatives are especially vulnerable to offense because creativity requires vulnerability. Writers, artists, musicians, speakers, dancers, filmmakers, and visionaries often pour pieces of themselves into what they create. Rejection can feel deeply personal. Criticism can feel painful. Being overlooked can feel devastating.

If creatives do not heal properly, offense can silence their voice, bury their gift, and distort their purpose.

Many creatives stopped creating because bitterness convinced them nobody cared. Others became resentful because they felt unsupported, mishandled, dishonored, or overlooked.

But offense cannot be allowed to bury your assignment. Your gift is too important to surrender to bitterness, comparison, or emotional pain.

How to Crush the Giant of Offense

EXPOSE THE ROOT

Healing begins with honesty. Ask God to reveal the true source of the offense. Sometimes the issue is deeper than the present situation. Sometimes old wounds are reacting through current pain. You cannot heal what you refuse to confront.

CHOOSE FORGIVENESS

Forgiveness does not mean what happened was acceptable. Forgiveness means you refuse to allow bitterness to continue poisoning your heart. Ephesians 4 commands believers to put away bitterness, wrath, anger, and malice. Healing cannot grow where bitterness is continually fed.

RECEIVE CORRECTION WITH HUMILITY

Mature people understand that correction is often protection. Every correction is not rejection. Sometimes God uses truth, leadership, accountability, and difficult conversations to expose areas that still require growth and healing.

Wise people grow through correction. Prideful people become offended by it.

STOP REHEARSING THE WOUND

Whatever you continually replay emotionally becomes stronger spiritually. Many people repeatedly rehearse conversations, betrayals, disappointments, and offenses until bitterness becomes rooted deeply within them. Stop feeding the wound. Feed your spirit instead.

GUARD YOUR HEART

Proverbs 4:23 says to guard your heart diligently because the issues of life flow from it. If your heart becomes poisoned, your relationships, leadership, communication, creativity, and spiritual life eventually become poisoned too. Protect your heart intentionally.

PURSUE RECONCILIATION

Jesus taught believers to pursue reconciliation quickly. Healthy communication prevents division from deepening. Many relationships could be restored if people confronted offense with humility, maturity, honesty, and love instead of silence, pride, and avoidance.

Prayer

Father, in the name of Jesus, I ask You to search my heart and expose every root of offense hidden within me. Reveal every place where bitterness, resentment, pride, jealousy, anger, unforgiveness, rejection, insecurity, or emotional pain has taken root. Heal every wound that has distorted my perception, damaged my relationships, affected my leadership, silenced my creativity, or poisoned my heart. Forgive me for every time I allowed offense to grow instead of bringing my pain before You.

Lord, deliver me from spiritual blindness. Remove every hardened place in my heart. Tear down every wall built from disappointment, betrayal, hurt, rejection, correction, abandonment, or misunderstanding. Teach me to respond with wisdom instead of reaction, humility instead of pride, and maturity instead of emotional toxicity. Help me not to magnify every offense, replay every wound, or assume the worst about others.

Father, I renounce every trap of Satan connected to offense, division, bitterness, jealousy, resentment, suspicion, competition, and unforgiveness. I refuse to allow offense to separate me from healthy relationships, godly accountability, spiritual leadership, or divine purpose. Heal my emotions. Heal my mind. Heal my heart. Restore my ability to trust, love, forgive, communicate, and walk in unity.

I declare that offense will not control me. Bitterness will not poison me. Pride will not rule me. Emotional wounds will not define me. I will not remain trapped by pain. I choose freedom. I choose healing. I choose forgiveness. I choose spiritual maturity. Let my heart remain pure before You. In Jesus' name, amen.

DECLARATIONS

- I will not be trapped by offense.
- I refuse bitterness, resentment, division, pride, and emotional toxicity.
- Every root of bitterness is uprooted from my life.
- I will not allow pain to distort my perception.
- I choose healing over hurt and freedom over bondage.
- I will not rehearse wounds, replay pain, or magnify offenses.
- My heart will remain pure before God.
- I receive correction with humility, wisdom, and maturity.
- I refuse to be hypersensitive, defensive, suspicious, or emotionally reactive.

- I will not isolate myself from healthy relationships or godly accountability.
- I choose forgiveness even when my flesh wants revenge.
- I release every person who hurt, rejected, betrayed, disappointed, abandoned, or offended me.
- I refuse to celebrate the failures of others.
- I will walk in unity, humility, love, emotional health, and spiritual maturity.
- My wounds will not silence my purpose.
- My pain will not poison my future.
- I will not allow offense to destroy my leadership, ministry, family, creativity, or relationships.
- I renounce every spirit of division, bitterness, jealousy, pride, and unforgiveness.
- I walk in healing.

- I walk in wisdom.
- I walk in discernment.
- I walk in love.
- I walk in freedom.

I crush the giant of offense in Jesus' name.

ENTITLEMENT

Scriptures

James 4:6, Philippians 2:3–5, Matthew 20:26–28, Luke 17:10, Proverbs 16:18, Galatians 6:9, Ecclesiastes 3:11, Romans 12:3, Colossians 3:23, 1 Peter 5:5–6

Meet the Giant

Entitlement is one of the most deceptive giants in the land. Unlike rejection, fear, anxiety, or grief, entitlement rarely introduces itself by name. Few people wake up believing they struggle with entitlement. Instead, it disguises itself as disappointment, offense, comparison, frustration, resentment, pride, or the feeling that life has somehow treated them unfairly. Because it wears so many different masks, it often goes unnoticed until it has already begun shaping the way a person thinks, relates to others, and even relates to God.

At its core, entitlement is the belief that you deserve something simply because you desire it, have waited long enough for it, or believe your past experiences have earned it. It is the expectation of reward without responsibility. It is the expectation of harvest without sowing. It is the expectation of promotion without preparation. It is the expectation of honor without service. It quietly shifts our focus from stewardship to deservingness.

The giant whispers subtle messages that sound reasonable on the surface: "I deserve better." "They owe me." "It's my turn." "After everything I've done, someone should recognize me." "I shouldn't have to go through this." Over time, these thoughts become more than passing frustrations. They become beliefs that influence our attitudes, our relationships, and our responses whenever life fails to meet our expectations.

It is important to distinguish entitlement from healthy confidence.

God never intended His children to live with poor self-esteem or a diminished sense of worth. Knowing your value is not entitlement. Understanding your identity in Christ is not entitlement. Expecting God to remain faithful to His promises is not entitlement. Healthy confidence is rooted in who God says you are. Entitlement is rooted in what you believe others owe you.

Entitlement begins the moment expectation becomes demand. It begins when gratitude quietly leaves the room and is replaced with the assumption that blessings are obligations rather than gifts. The entitled heart gradually stops appreciating what it has because it becomes consumed with what it believes it should have.

One of the greatest dangers of this giant is that it blinds us to itself. We can often recognize entitlement in a coworker, a family member, a leader, or even a stranger while remaining completely unaware of its influence in our own lives. Like pride, entitlement hides behind seemingly reasonable thoughts and emotions. It convinces us that our expectations are always justified, our disappointments are always someone else's fault, and our frustrations are always evidence that we have been treated unfairly.

If left unchecked, entitlement slowly erodes humility, weakens gratitude, damages relationships, and creates chronic dissatisfaction. No amount of success, recognition, wealth, or opportunity can satisfy a heart that continually believes it deserves more.

That is why this giant must be confronted. Until entitlement is exposed, it will continue stealing joy, distorting purpose, and preventing us from appreciating the grace of God.

What Is Entitlement Clinically?

From a clinical perspective, entitlement is most commonly described as **psychological entitlement**, a personality characteristic and cognitive pattern in which an individual believes they deserve more privileges, recognition, opportunities, resources, or favorable treatment than others regardless of effort, responsibility, reciprocity, or circumstances. Although entitlement is not classified as a mental disorder in the *Diagnostic and Statistical Manual of Mental Disorders (DSM-5)*, it has been widely studied because of its significant impact on emotional health, relationships, leadership, workplace functioning, and overall life satisfaction.

Researchers have found that psychological entitlement is often associated with unrealistic expectations, chronic dissatisfaction, difficulty accepting correction, lower empathy, increased interpersonal conflict, and reduced gratitude. Ironically, people with a stronger sense of entitlement often report lower levels of satisfaction because their expectations consistently exceed reality. The wider the gap between what they expect and what actually happens, the greater their disappointment, frustration, resentment, and offense.

Clinically, entitlement is also influenced by what psychologists refer to as **cognitive schemas**, deeply held beliefs that shape how we interpret everyday experiences. These mental frameworks develop over time through our upbringing, relationships, personal experiences, successes, disappointments, and repeated patterns of thinking. Once those schemas are established, the brain begins filtering new experiences through them.

For example, a person whose internal belief is, "People should always recognize my efforts," will naturally interpret a lack of recognition as rejection or injustice. Another person whose internal belief is, "I deserve special treatment because of everything I've been through," may perceive ordinary boundaries or healthy accountability as disrespect or unfairness. The situation may not actually be unjust, but the mind has already interpreted it through an entitled lens.

Neuroscience reminds us that repeated thoughts strengthen neural pathways within the brain. Every time we rehearse thoughts such as, "They owe me," "This isn't fair," "I deserve better," or "Someone should have taken care of this," those pathways become increasingly automatic. Eventually, the brain begins interpreting ordinary disappointments as personal offenses without conscious effort. This is one reason Scripture repeatedly emphasizes the renewing of the mind. Romans 12:2 is not simply spiritual language. It describes a process of replacing unhealthy patterns of thinking with truth until our minds are transformed.

Another important clinical concept connected to entitlement is **low frustration tolerance**. Individuals with low frustration tolerance often struggle to regulate their emotions when life does not unfold according to their expectations. Minor inconveniences may produce disproportionately large emotional reactions because internally they believe things should have happened differently. What appears to others as an overreaction is often the result of unrealistic expectations colliding with reality.

Although entitlement is frequently associated with narcissistic traits, the two are not identical. Narcissistic Personality Disorder includes entitlement as one of its characteristics, but many emotionally healthy individuals can still develop entitled patterns of thinking without meeting the criteria for a personality disorder. Entitlement exists on a spectrum. It can emerge during seasons of success, prolonged comfort, comparison, overindulgence, pride, or even repeated disappointment.

One of the most overlooked aspects of entitlement is that it is not always born out of arrogance. Sometimes it grows out of unresolved pain.

A child who was constantly overlooked may grow into an adult who demands attention. Someone who experienced chronic rejection may begin believing the world owes them acceptance. A person who endured years of deprivation may unconsciously expect everyone around them to compensate for what they never received. Others develop entitlement because they were rarely told "no," consistently rescued from consequences, or praised without being challenged to grow.

These experiences help explain how entitlement develops, but they do not excuse it. Understanding the origin of a giant is not the same as surrendering to it. Healing begins when we honestly acknowledge both the wound beneath the entitlement and the unhealthy expectations that have grown from it.

This is where psychology and Scripture beautifully complement one another. Clinical research helps us understand how entitlement develops within the mind, emotions, and relationships. Scripture reveals how God transforms the heart. Psychology explains the pattern. The Holy Spirit empowers the change.

The Bible consistently calls us to renew our minds, cultivate humility, embrace gratitude, and become faithful stewards rather than demanding consumers. As our thinking changes, our expectations change. As our expectations change, our relationships improve. As our hearts become more grateful, entitlement loses its influence.

The goal is not simply to manage entitled behavior. The goal is to become the kind of person whose heart is so overwhelmed by God's grace that gratitude naturally replaces the belief that anyone owes us anything.

How Do You Know You Are Fighting the Giant of Entitlement?

One of the greatest dangers of entitlement is that it often feels justified. Unlike fear, anxiety, or anger, entitlement rarely announces itself as a problem. Instead, it disguises itself as fairness. It convinces us that our expectations are reasonable, our disappointments are deserved, and our frustrations are someone else's fault. Because of this, many people struggle with entitlement for years without ever recognizing it.

Entitlement is not always loud or arrogant. Sometimes it is quiet. It can hide behind hurt, disappointment, exhaustion, comparison, or the belief that life has been unfair. It often sounds less like, "I'm better than everyone else," and more like, "After everything I've been through, I deserve better."

One of the clearest signs that entitlement is influencing your life is becoming easily offended when people fail to respond the way you expected. Perhaps someone failed to acknowledge your hard work, include you in an opportunity, return your kindness, or recognize your sacrifice. While disappointment is a normal part of life, entitlement quietly transforms disappointment into resentment because it convinces you that you were owed something rather than simply hoping for it.

You may also be battling entitlement if you regularly expect people to anticipate your needs without healthy communication. Instead of expressing what you need, you assume that people should already know. When they fail to meet those unspoken expectations, frustration begins to grow. Healthy relationships are built on communication. Entitlement often replaces communication with assumption.

Another warning sign is difficulty celebrating other people's success. Rather than rejoicing when someone else is promoted, recognized, or blessed, you quietly begin comparing your life to theirs. Their victory feels like your loss. Their opportunity feels like evidence that you have been overlooked. Comparison is one of entitlement's closest companions because it continually measures what someone else has instead of appreciating what God has already entrusted to you.

Entitlement also appears when we expect honor without service, promotion without preparation, influence without contribution, or blessing without stewardship. Instead of asking, "How can I continue growing?" the entitled heart asks, "Why haven't they recognized me yet?" Growth becomes secondary to recognition, and recognition becomes the measure of success.

Correction is another revealing test. If constructive feedback consistently feels like rejection, accountability feels like a personal attack, or healthy boundaries feel disrespectful, entitlement may be operating beneath the surface. Humility welcomes correction because it sees it as an opportunity to grow. Entitlement resists correction because it believes it has already earned acceptance.

One of the strongest clinical indicators of entitlement is what psychologists describe as low frustration tolerance. Individuals with low frustration tolerance often experience intense emotional reactions when circumstances fail to meet their expectations. Small inconveniences may trigger disproportionate anger, offense, discouragement, or withdrawal because internally they believe things should have unfolded differently. The issue is often not the event itself but the expectation attached to it.

Research also suggests that individuals with higher levels of psychological entitlement frequently struggle with emotional regulation during disappointment. Instead of adapting to unexpected circumstances, they are more likely to become offended, blame others, or interpret ordinary setbacks as personal injustices. This helps explain why some people remain emotionally stuck after relatively minor disappointments while others recover more quickly. The difference is often found in the expectations they carried into the situation.

Perhaps the greatest evidence of entitlement is chronic complaint. When gratitude decreases, entitlement usually increases. A person can be surrounded by answered prayers, healthy relationships, opportunities, and blessings yet remain dissatisfied because entitlement continually directs attention toward what is missing rather than what has already been received.

There is also a relational cost to entitlement. Clinical research consistently shows that unrealistic expectations often contribute to conflict, decreased relationship satisfaction, poor communication, blame shifting, and reduced empathy. Healthy relationships ask, "How can I love, serve, and understand you?" Entitlement asks, "Why aren't you loving, serving, and understanding me?"

That does not mean having needs is wrong. God created us for healthy relationships, mutual care, and emotional connection. The problem begins when expectations become demands and appreciation is replaced with assumption.

The good news is that recognizing entitlement is not a reason for shame. It is an invitation to freedom. God never exposes a giant to embarrass us. He exposes it so He can help us overcome it. Every area He reveals is another area He desires to heal.

The Princess Effect

One expression of entitlement is what I call the Princess Effect. The Princess Effect is when a person embraces the language of royalty but forgets the responsibilities that accompany it. It is the mindset that says, "Because I am special, I should be treated as special everywhere I go," regardless of the environment, the relationship, the circumstances, or the expectations placed upon them.

Let me be clear. There is absolutely nothing wrong with knowing your worth. There is nothing wrong with understanding that you are fearfully and wonderfully made. There is nothing wrong with believing you are loved by God, chosen by Him, and created with purpose. Every believer should understand their identity in Christ.

The problem begins when identity becomes entitlement.

One of the greatest strategies of this giant is that it twists a biblical truth into an unhealthy expectation. Scripture teaches that we are sons and daughters of the King. We are heirs with Christ. We have been adopted into God's family. Those truths should produce confidence, humility, gratitude, and security. Instead, entitlement distorts those truths until a person begins believing everyone else exists to affirm them, accommodate them, protect them, and revolve around them.

A princess belongs to a kingdom, but she is also accountable to that kingdom. Royalty is not simply about privilege. It is about responsibility. It requires maturity, discipline, wisdom, service, and representing the values of the kingdom well.

The Princess Effect removes the responsibility while demanding the privilege. It wants the crown without the character. The title without the training. The influence without the integrity. The blessing without the burden. The platform without the preparation. The reward without the process.

This mindset often appears in relationships. A person expects constant pursuit, constant affirmation, constant apologies, and constant accommodation while offering very little self-examination in return. They expect patience but struggle to extend patience. They desire grace but withhold grace. They want to be understood while making very little effort to understand others.

Imagine a woman wearing a tiara and crown to a baseball game because she sees herself as a princess. There is nothing inherently wrong with the crown. The problem is discernment. What may be appropriate in one setting becomes distracting and out of place in another.

Entitlement functions the same way. It causes people to overdress emotionally for environments that require humility.

They bring a throne mentality into a team environment.

They expect royal treatment in places where cooperation, flexibility, accountability, and mutual respect are required.

Instead of asking, “How can I contribute?” they quietly begin asking, “How should everyone treat me?”

The Princess Effect also influences attitude. A person may believe they should be free to say whatever they want, ignore healthy boundaries, avoid accountability, or refuse correction while still expecting to be handled delicately and honored highly. They desire freedom without responsibility, privilege without accountability, and favor without faithfulness.

This mindset can even affect our relationship with God. Instead of approaching Him with gratitude, we begin approaching Him with demands. Prayer slowly shifts from surrender to expectation. We become frustrated when God does not answer according to our timeline or fulfill our plans exactly as we imagined them.

The danger of the Princess Effect is that it confuses worth with worship. You deserve dignity. You deserve respect. You deserve to be treated as someone created in the image of God. But no one is called to worship you. No one is called to revolve around your preferences. No one is responsible for carrying the weight of expectations that only God can satisfy.

True royalty always carries responsibility. In God's Kingdom, sons and daughters do not simply wear crowns. They also carry crosses. They serve. They submit. They forgive. They honor others. They embrace humility. They understand that being chosen does not excuse immaturity and that being valuable does not entitle them to special treatment.

Kingdom identity never produces arrogance. It produces gratitude. It produces humility. It produces servant leadership. And ultimately, it produces a heart that looks more like Jesus.

What Entitlement Looks Like Today

Although the biblical examples of entitlement took place thousands of years ago, this giant has not changed. It has simply adapted to modern culture. Today, entitlement quietly influences marriages, families, churches, businesses, schools, friendships, ministries, and even our relationship with God. It often disguises itself as confidence, self-care, fairness, ambition, or simply "knowing my worth." While there is certainly a place for healthy confidence and appropriate boundaries, entitlement crosses the line when appreciation is replaced with expectation and expectation becomes demand.

One reason entitlement has become increasingly difficult to recognize is because modern culture often celebrates individual rights while minimizing personal responsibility. We are constantly encouraged to pursue what we deserve, demand what belongs to us, and refuse anything that feels uncomfortable. Although there are certainly times when justice should be pursued and healthy boundaries established, entitlement teaches us to focus almost exclusively on what others owe us rather than on what we owe God and one another.

Because of this, entitlement quietly reshapes the way people think, communicate, lead, work, worship, and build relationships.

Relational Entitlement

Relationships are one of the first places entitlement reveals itself. Healthy relationships are built upon mutual love, sacrifice, communication, forgiveness, and shared responsibility. Entitlement slowly replaces those qualities with unrealistic expectations.

Instead of asking, "How can I love you?" entitlement asks, "Why aren't you loving me the way I deserve?" Instead of asking, "How can I serve?" it asks, "Why am I not being served?" Instead of communicating needs with humility, entitlement assumes other people should already know what we need.

Clinical research consistently shows that unrealistic expectations contribute to conflict, lower relationship satisfaction, poor communication, blame shifting, reduced empathy, and difficulty compromising. When one or both people believe the relationship exists primarily to meet their needs, disappointment becomes inevitable.

Many marital conflicts, family disagreements, workplace tensions, and fractured friendships are not caused by a lack of love. They are fueled by expectations that were never communicated, expectations that were unrealistic, or expectations that gradually became demands.

The healthiest relationships are built on mutual service rather than mutual scorekeeping.

Workplace Entitlement

Entitlement also appears in the workplace. It expects promotions without preparation. Influence without contribution. Authority without accountability. Recognition without excellence.

Instead of focusing on becoming more valuable, the entitled employee often becomes preoccupied with being more visible. They measure success by titles rather than by growth, responsibility, and consistent excellence.

Psychologists have found that individuals with higher levels of entitlement often become discouraged more quickly when recognition is delayed because they believe their effort should automatically produce immediate reward.

Kingdom thinking teaches something very different.

Faithfulness precedes promotion. Excellence creates opportunity. Character sustains influence. God often develops the person long before He enlarges the platform.

Ministry Entitlement

Few places are more vulnerable to entitlement than ministry. Ministry is built upon serving others, yet entitlement quietly transforms ministry into a pursuit of position instead of purpose.

A person begins expecting a title because they have attended faithfully. They expect a platform because they are gifted. They expect influence because they have been waiting. They expect authority while resisting accountability.

The danger is subtle because many of these desires are not wrong by themselves. The problem arises when the desire becomes a demand.

Throughout Scripture, God consistently developed character before assigning greater responsibility. David served before he ruled. Joseph endured hardship before he governed. Elisha served Elijah before receiving his mantle. Jesus spent years preparing before beginning His public ministry. God has never confused gifting with readiness. Neither should we.

Spiritual Entitlement

Perhaps the most dangerous form of entitlement is spiritual entitlement because it affects the way we relate to God Himself.

Spiritual entitlement expects God to bless decisions He never approved. It expects promises without obedience. Harvest without sowing. Victory without discipline. Maturity without surrender.

Sometimes people become frustrated because they believe that years of church attendance, faithful service, generous giving, or sincere prayer obligate God to answer every request according to their preferred timeline. But God cannot be manipulated. He is gracious, but He is not obligated.

Everything He gives flows from His wisdom, His love, and His perfect timing. Grace is never something we earn. It is always something we receive.

What Entitlement Looks Like in Leaders

Leadership amplifies whatever already exists within the heart. If humility is present, influence expands humility. If entitlement is present, influence expands entitlement. That is why entitlement is particularly dangerous for leaders.

Healthy leaders view leadership as stewardship.

Entitled leaders begin treating leadership as ownership. They slowly move from serving people to expecting people to serve them. They may begin believing their position exempts them from accountability. They resist correction because they assume experience has eliminated the need for growth. They expect loyalty while offering very little transparency. They seek honor more than service.

Leadership research has consistently shown that leaders with elevated feelings of entitlement are often more resistant to feedback, more likely to externalize blame, and less willing to acknowledge mistakes. Because entitlement creates blind spots, these leaders frequently overestimate their own effectiveness while underestimating the value of others. This explains why Scripture repeatedly emphasizes humility in leadership.

Jesus, the greatest leader who ever lived, consistently modeled servant leadership. He washed feet. He welcomed children. He touched lepers. He served those who could offer Him nothing in return.

Matthew 20:28 declares, "Even as the Son of man came not to be ministered unto, but to minister, and to give his life a ransom for many."

If the King chose a towel instead of a throne, no leader is ever above serving.

What Entitlement Looks Like in Creatives

Creatives often experience entitlement differently because creativity is deeply connected to identity.

Writers, artists, musicians, entrepreneurs, filmmakers, speakers, pastors, designers, and visionaries pour pieces of themselves into what they create. Because creative work is personal, rejection often feels personal as well.

Without realizing it, the desire for encouragement can slowly become the expectation of recognition.

The giant begins whispering:

"People don't appreciate your gift." "You deserve a larger platform." "They should support everything you create." "Someone else is succeeding because you've been overlooked."

Comparison begins replacing stewardship. Validation begins replacing purpose.

Research on creativity consistently demonstrates that creative individuals often tie their personal identity closely to their work. When that identity becomes overly dependent upon external validation, disappointment can easily become discouragement, bitterness, or entitlement.

God never intended your identity to rest in your platform. Your identity rests in Christ. Your platform is simply an assignment. Talent may open a door. Character keeps it open. Gifting may attract attention. Humility sustains influence.

God is often far more interested in developing the vessel than expanding the audience.

The Cost of Entitlement

Every giant steals something. Entitlement is no exception. It steals gratitude because nothing ever feels like enough. It steals joy because expectations continually exceed reality. It steals relationships because demands eventually replace love. It steals teachability because correction begins to feel offensive. It steals opportunities because pride resists the very growth that promotion requires. It steals purpose because it convinces people they should already possess what God is still preparing them to steward.

Perhaps most tragically, entitlement steals intimacy with God. The entitled heart spends so much time focusing on what has not yet been received that it loses sight of the God who has already given so much.

The giant promises satisfaction but delivers chronic disappointment. It promises significance but produces isolation. It promises honor but ultimately leads to humiliation.

That is why entitlement must be confronted. Until it is surrendered, it will quietly sabotage every area of life. But when humility takes its place, gratitude returns. Relationships begin to heal. Purpose becomes clearer. Joy is restored. And the heart once again recognizes every blessing as an undeserved gift of God's amazing grace.

How to Crush the Giant of Entitlement

Every giant can be defeated, but no giant falls by accident. Just as David intentionally selected five smooth stones before facing Goliath, we must intentionally develop the attitudes, habits, and spiritual disciplines that weaken entitlement and strengthen humility.

The good news is that entitlement is not your identity. It is a mindset that can be renewed, a pattern that can be broken, and a giant that can be crushed through the transforming power of God's Word, the work of the Holy Spirit, and daily choices that align our hearts with His.

Crushing the giant of entitlement begins with recognizing that the battle is not primarily against other people. It is a battle within our own hearts. We are not fighting people who failed to meet our expectations. We are confronting the expectations that have quietly replaced our gratitude.

Develop a Lifestyle of Gratitude

Gratitude is one of the greatest weapons against entitlement because gratitude continually reminds us that every good gift comes from God.

Entitlement asks, "Why haven't I received more?"

Gratitude asks, "How have I already been blessed?"

Research in positive psychology consistently demonstrates that grateful people tend to experience greater emotional well-being, stronger relationships, increased resilience, lower levels of depression, greater life satisfaction, and higher levels of empathy. Gratitude changes the way people interpret their experiences. Instead of focusing on what is absent, grateful people learn to recognize what is already present.

Long before psychologists studied gratitude, Scripture revealed its transforming power.

The Apostle Paul repeatedly instructed believers to give thanks in every circumstance, not because every circumstance is good, but because gratitude keeps our hearts anchored in God's faithfulness rather than our changing circumstances.

A practical way to cultivate gratitude is to intentionally record God's blessings each day. When you regularly remember His faithfulness, entitlement loses its ability to convince you that God has somehow forgotten you.

Embrace Personal Responsibility

Entitlement shifts responsibility outward.

Growth brings responsibility inward.

One of the most transformative questions you can ask yourself is, "What is my responsibility in this situation?"

That question changes everything.

Instead of blaming circumstances, waiting on other people, or focusing on what you cannot control, you begin taking ownership of what God has entrusted to you.

Psychologists have long recognized that people who develop an internal sense of responsibility tend to demonstrate greater resilience, stronger problem-solving skills, and healthier emotional functioning than those who consistently believe their lives are controlled by outside forces.

Scripture teaches the same principle. God consistently blesses faithful stewardship. Before David ruled a nation, he faithfully tended sheep. Before Joseph managed Egypt, he faithfully managed a prison. Before God enlarges our assignment, He often examines how we handle our current one. Promotion follows stewardship.

Replace Comparison with Celebration

Comparison is one of entitlement's greatest allies.

The moment we begin measuring our lives against someone else's journey, dissatisfaction quietly begins to grow.

Comparison whispers, "Why them?" Celebration declares, "Thank You, Lord, for blessing them."

Celebrating others does not diminish your future. It

demonstrates trust in God's sovereignty. Every person's assignment is different. Every timeline is different. Every calling is different. Someone else's blessing is not evidence that God has forgotten you.

Learning to celebrate another person's success is one of the clearest indicators that gratitude is replacing entitlement.

Serve Without Seeking Recognition

Jesus completely redefined greatness. The world says greatness is being served. Jesus said greatness is serving.

Entitlement constantly asks, "Who notices me?"

Humility quietly asks, "Who can I help?"

One of the fastest ways to weaken entitlement is to intentionally serve where there is little applause. Serve without the microphone. Serve without the title. Serve without social media recognition. Serve without expecting repayment.

Every unseen act of obedience strengthens humility and weakens the giant's influence.

When service becomes your lifestyle instead of your strategy for recognition, your heart begins looking more like Christ.

Trust God's Process and His Timing

Many struggles with entitlement are actually struggles with timing.

We become frustrated because we believe we should already have what God is still preparing us to steward.

Ecclesiastes 3:11 reminds us that God "hath made every thing beautiful in his time."

Notice that Scripture does not merely say God makes things beautiful. It says He makes them beautiful in His time.

Waiting is never wasted when God is using it to develop your character. The process often prepares us for the very blessing we are praying to receive.

David's years as a shepherd prepared him for the palace. Joseph's prison prepared him for leadership. Moses' wilderness prepared him to lead a nation. Jesus' hidden years prepared Him for public ministry.

If God trusted the process with them, we can trust His process for us.

Remember That Everything Is Grace

Perhaps the greatest cure for entitlement is remembering grace. Grace reminds us that God does not deal with us according to what we deserve. He deals with us according to His mercy.

Every breath is grace. Every opportunity is grace. Every relationship is grace. Every open door is grace. Every answered prayer is grace. Even unanswered prayers are often expressions of grace because God sees what we cannot.

The more we understand grace, the more gratitude grows.

The more gratitude grows, the weaker entitlement becomes.

Remain Teachable

Entitlement resists correction. Humility welcomes it.

One of the greatest signs of spiritual maturity is remaining teachable regardless of age, experience, education, or position.

Ask God to reveal blind spots. Invite trusted people to speak truth into your life. Receive correction without becoming defensive.

Growth rarely happens inside our comfort zone. It often begins the moment we become willing to hear what we did not want to hear.

A teachable heart is a protected heart.

Renew Your Mind Daily

Because entitlement develops through repeated patterns of thinking, it must also be defeated through repeated patterns of truth.

Romans 12:2 reminds us to "be transformed by the renewing of your mind."

Transformation is not a one-time event. It is a daily decision.

Each time you replace complaint with thanksgiving... Comparison with celebration...Demand with surrender...Pride with humility...

You are weakening old neural pathways while strengthening new patterns of thinking rooted in God's truth. As your mind is renewed, your expectations change. As your expectations change, your relationships become healthier. As your relationships become healthier, your heart becomes freer.

God is not merely changing your behavior. He is transforming the way you think. That transformation is what ultimately crushes the giant of entitlement.

Giant-Killing Truths

- Entitlement grows where gratitude is forgotten.
- Humility is the antidote to pride.
- Grace reminds me that everything I have is a gift from God.
- Stewardship always precedes promotion.
- Service is the pathway to significance.
- Comparison blinds me to my own blessings.
- God's timing is preparing me for God's purpose.
- Character sustains what talent attracts.
- No one owes me my purpose. My responsibility is to faithfully steward what God has entrusted to me.

- The process is not punishment. It is preparation.
- The greatest among us are still servants.

One of the most important truths about entitlement is this: entitlement is often the hidden giant behind offense. Whenever bitterness, resentment, chronic disappointment, or offense begin taking root, it is wise to prayerfully ask, "What expectation have I elevated above God's grace?" That question often exposes the very place where this giant has been hiding.

Prayer for Crushing Entitlement

Father, in the name of Jesus, I come before You with a humble heart. Search me and know me. Reveal every area where pride, selfishness, comparison, offense, or entitlement has taken root within me.

Forgive me for the times I have focused more on what I believed I deserved than on the countless blessings You have already placed in my life. Thank You for Your mercy, Your patience, and Your amazing grace.

Teach me to be grateful in every season. Help me to celebrate the victories of others without comparison and to trust Your timing without frustration. Give me the heart of a servant and the mind of Christ.

Renew my thinking where entitlement has distorted my perspective. Heal every wound that has caused me to expect people to give what only You can provide. Remove every spirit of pride, offense, selfish ambition, and self-centeredness that would hinder my growth and my relationship with You.

Help me embrace responsibility, welcome correction, and faithfully steward every opportunity You place before me. Let humility become my strength, gratitude become my lifestyle, and grace become the lens through which I see every blessing.

I declare that this giant will not control my future. Through the power of the Holy Spirit, I choose humility over pride, gratitude over complaint, service over self-promotion, and surrender over selfish ambition.

In Jesus' name, Amen.

Declarations for Crushing Entitlement

- I recognize that every good gift in my life comes from God.
- I choose gratitude over complaint.
- I reject every spirit of entitlement.
- I embrace humility, responsibility, and faithful stewardship.
- I celebrate the success of others with genuine joy.
- I trust God's process and His perfect timing.
- I will serve with excellence whether anyone notices or not.
- My identity is found in Christ, not in recognition or position.

often the struggle to believe His promises in the middle of painful circumstances. We learned that faith is strengthened as we choose to trust God's character, even when we do not yet understand His timing.

We exposed the giant of **anxiety**, discovering that fear about tomorrow can rob us of the peace God desires us to experience today. Anxiety attempts to magnify uncertainty, but God's presence always remains greater than our circumstances. His peace still guards hearts and minds that are surrendered to Him.

We examined the giant of **loneliness** and discovered that being alone and feeling alone are not the same thing. Loneliness often whispers lies about our value, our purpose, and our place, but God reminds us that He will never leave us nor forsake us. He is present even in seasons when His presence seems difficult to feel.

We challenged the giant of **rebellion**, understanding that rebellion is not always loud or obvious. Sometimes it appears as delayed obedience, partial obedience, pride, self-will, or resisting the very direction that leads to freedom. Yet every step of surrender brings us closer to God's purpose for our lives.

We confronted the giant of **offense**, one of the enemy's most subtle yet destructive weapons. Offense quietly imprisons the one carrying it. Left unresolved, it hardens the heart, poisons relationships, clouds discernment, and limits spiritual growth. Freedom begins when we choose forgiveness, even when forgiveness is difficult.

Finally, we exposed the giant of **entitlement**, one of the most deceptive giants of all. Entitlement convinces us that we deserve what we have not prepared for, that others owe us what only God can provide, or that our expectations should outweigh His process. It breeds disappointment, comparison, resentment, pride, and offense. Yet the Kingdom of God is built upon humility, gratitude, stewardship, service, and surrender. As we exchange entitlement for thankfulness and trust, we position ourselves to receive God's blessings His way and in His timing.

Each of these giants may look different, but they all have one thing in common. They seek to separate you from the abundant life God has prepared for you. They seek to influence your thinking, your relationships, your decisions, your purpose, and your destiny. Yet every giant we have studied has already met its match in Jesus Christ. Through His finished work, every stronghold can be broken, every wound can be healed, every chain can be shattered, and every giant can be crushed.

Remember, the goal has never been simply to defeat your giants. The goal is to crush them so thoroughly that they no longer govern your thoughts, direct your decisions, or determine your future. Defeating a giant may win a battle, but crushing a giant changes a life. As you continue your journey, remain watchful. Giants often return wearing different faces, but the principles you have learned throughout this series will help you recognize them before they regain influence. Continue walking in truth. Continue renewing your mind. Continue allowing the Holy Spirit to heal every hidden place. Continue choosing obedience over compromise, faith over fear, forgiveness over offense, and hope over despair.

This volume is only one part of the larger *Crushing the Giants* journey. Every volume is designed to expose different giants, provide biblical understanding, practical application, ministry principles, and personal reflection to help you experience lasting transformation. Together, the series addresses the spiritual, emotional, clinical, and practical dimensions of overcoming the battles that seek to limit God's people.

If this is your first *Crushing the Giants* book, I encourage you to continue the journey by exploring the other volumes in the series. Each volume builds upon the same biblical foundation while addressing additional giants that influence our lives, relationships, emotions, purpose, and spiritual growth. As you continue reading, you will develop an even deeper understanding of how giants operate, how they are formed, and how God empowers His people to overcome them.

Be sure to explore the *Crushing the Giants* Youth Edition, written specifically to help teenagers identify and overcome the battles they face during one of life's most formative seasons. Young people today are confronting challenges unlike any previous generation, and they need practical, biblical tools to recognize the giants that seek to shape their identity and future before those giants become lifelong strongholds.

Don't forget the *Crushing the Giants* Children's Edition, designed to introduce young hearts and minds to biblical courage, obedience, perseverance, kindness, and faith through engaging stories that teach children they can trust God in every circumstance. The greatest victories often begin with the lessons we learn while we are still young.

Whether you are reading these books personally, studying with your family, leading a small group, counseling others, teaching a class, or equipping leaders, my prayer is that this series becomes more than something you read. I pray it becomes something you live.

The battle is real, but so is the victory. Your past does not determine your future. Your wounds do not define your identity. Your failures do not cancel your purpose. Your giants do not decide your destiny. God does.

Stand firm in His promises. Walk boldly in His truth. Refuse to surrender ground that Christ has already won for you. Keep digging the wells of faith. Keep renewing your mind. Keep trusting His Word. Keep advancing toward everything He has promised.

Most importantly, never forget that giants are not proof that God has abandoned you. More often, they are evidence that you are standing at the edge of something greater than you have yet experienced. Every giant is an invitation to discover the greatness of the God who fights for you.

Thank you for allowing me to walk with you through this portion of your journey. I count it a privilege to encourage, equip, and challenge you as you pursue the life God has called you to live.

To learn more about the entire *Crushing the Giants* series, discover additional resources, connect with future releases, and continue your journey toward lasting freedom, visit **CrushingTheGiants.com**.

Now go forward with confidence.
Walk in healing. Walk in freedom.
Walk in purpose. Walk in faith.

And above all else...

Keep crushing giants.

Dr. Renetta S. Watson is an author, educator,

and transformational leader with over 35 years in ministry, 26 years in leadership, and more than two decades equipping, preaching, and teaching across diverse communities. Known as "The Equipper," Dr. Watson carries a calling rooted in Ephesians 4 equipping leaders to walk in purpose, maturity, and Kingdom effectiveness. Her life focus and mandate are to impact communities, influence culture, and invoke lasting change. Equipper is not a title or brand, but a divine calling and mission.

Dr. Watson is also a Nationally Certified Christian Counselor, Church Consultant, and Christian Life Coach. In addition to her ministry work, Dr. Watson spent several years teaching high school mathematics and behavior specialist working with students in the juvenile justice system. Deeply committed to community transformation, Dr. Watson has served as a mentor, youth advocate, and community leader. She is the founder of EDUKATE Ministries, Equip Enterprises and Diamonds & Pearls Ministry.

Dr. Watson is also the author of Encouragement in the Storm, Developing Your Prayer Print, REAL8: Eight Principles for Healthy Relationships. The DREAM: A Blue Print for Evangelism & Discipleship,
SOAR: Strategies for Creating Systems that Build Healthy Churches, and Ministry: The Call You Can't Decline. She is co-author of Diamonds and Pearls: The Crown & Covenant.

www.CrushingTheGiants.com
www.WeBuildToSoar
www.AcaringTouchPublishing.com

www.ingramcontent.com/pod-product-compliance
Lightning Source LLC
LaVergne TN
LVHW040514210926
848480LV00005BA/1461
* 9 7 9 8 9 9 6 2 8 7 5 5 0 *